Under THE Olive Tree

Under THE Olive Tree

Italian Summer Food

MANUELA DARLING-GANSSER

Photography by Simon Griffiths

Hardie Grant Books

Acknowledgements

Many people have helped me in the preparation of this book. In Lugano my thanks especially, in so many ways, to my father Professor Augusto Gansser-Biaggi, to Luca and Gabi Gansser, Mario Gansser, zia Didi and zia Andi for their recollections of the Ristorante Biaggi and to Franco Serena.

In Sardegna my thanks go to Claudio and Barbera Biaggi, the ever-helpful Tito of Da Tito, Giovanni at Pietra Nieda, Susanne Aime, Mario Ragnedda and the late Dr Richard Fyfe.

My commissioning editor, Tracy O'Shaughnessy has encouraged and carefully guided the book, Klarissa Pfisterer has been a sympathetic and creative designer and Clare Coney has been a relentless text editor. Ros Ellis and Sue Reed have been diligent in typing the manuscript.

Maria Scarf and Judy Bell have made helpful suggestions.

Simon Griffiths has been excellent company on our travels and both professional and helpful in producing the marvellous photographs.

Above all, my thanks to my family who have inspired and encouraged the project from the outset. To my husband, Michele, particularly for his help with the text, and to my children Miranda, Jason and Daniel — I owe a special thanks. They have been my toughest critics and my biggest supporters.

Manuela
Sydney, August 2006

First published in 2003 by Hardie Grant Books
Paperback edition published in 2006
85 High Street, Prahran, Victoria 3181, Australia
www.hardiegrant.com.au

Cataloguing-in-Publication Data is available from the National Library of Australia
ISBN 1 74066 468 X
ISBN 978 1 74066 468 4

Edited by Clare Coney
Photography by Simon Griffiths
Cover and text design and layout by Pfisterer + Freeman
Printed and bound in Singapore by Imago Productions Pte. Ltd
10 9 8 7 6 5 4 3 2 1

Per La Mamma

Toti Gansser-Biaggi

1913–2000

Contents

Conversion Tables

WEIGHT

Metric	Imperial
10–15 g	½ oz
20 g	¾ oz
30 g	1 oz
40 g	1½ oz
50–60 g	2 oz
75 g	2½ oz
80 g	3 oz
100 g	3½ oz
125 g	4 oz
150 g	5 oz
175 g	6 oz
200 g	7 oz
225 g	8 oz
250 g	9 oz
275 g	10 oz
300 g	10½ oz
350 g	12 oz
400 g	14 oz
450 g	1 lb
500 g	1 lb 2 oz
600 g	1 lb 5 oz
650 g	1½ lb
750 g	1 lb 10 oz
900 g	2 lb
1 kg	2 lb 3 oz

VOLUME

Metric	Imperial
50–55 ml	2 fl oz
75 ml	3 fl oz
100 ml	3½ fl oz
120 ml	4 fl oz
150 ml	5 fl oz
170 ml	6 fl oz
200 ml	7 fl oz
225 ml	8 fl oz
250 ml	8½ fl oz
300 ml	10 fl oz
400 ml	13 fl oz
500 ml	17 fl oz
600 ml	20 fl oz
750 ml	25 fl oz
1 litre	34 fl oz

Note: A pint in the US contains 16 fl oz;
a pint in the UK contains 20 fl oz.

TEASPOONS, TABLESPOONS & CUPS

1 teaspoon	5 ml
1 tablespoon	20 ml
1 cup	250 ml

This book uses metric cup measurements, i.e. **250 ml for 1 cup**; in the US a cup is 8 fl oz, just smaller, and **American cooks should be generous** in their cup measurements; in the UK a cup is 10 fl oz and **British cooks should be scant** with their cup measurements.

TEMPERATURE

C°	F°
140	275
150	300
160	320
170	340
180	350
190	375
200	400
210	410
220	430

LENGTH

Metric	Imperial
5 mm	¼ in
1 cm	½ in
2 cm	¾ in
2.5 cm	1 in
5 cm	2 in
7.5 cm	3 in
10 cm	4 in
15 cm	6 in
20 cm	8 in
30 cm	12 in

Introduction

THIS BOOK BEGAN WHEN I SET OUT TO WRITE DOWN FOR MY THREE YOUNG adult children the family recipes – mine and those of previous generations. The project quickly took on a life of its own as I found that talking about the food was inseparable from the places and the people.

There have been serious cooks in our family for over 120 years, so what began as a simple exercise to write about food turned into a trip – for me very much a sentimental journey – to the sources of my personal inspiration. I decided to visit yet again the two places where it all began for me – Lugano and the Costa Smeralda. It is a story in words and pictures of what is special to me about these places, the people who have been part of my life and how I came to develop my personal preference for a relaxed and casual way of eating that went with the life we lived.

This life, at least in my memory, seems to be a time of endless summer. In my mind's eye we are eating outside on the terrace, 'al fresco' as the Italians call it, enjoying the food, the company and the magic of the setting. I have called this book *Under the Olive Tree* after the table in the garden under an ancient olive on the terrace at my family home in Lugano where it all began.

My travels centre on two places that are not really linked except in my life – Lugano, the elegant lakeside city in southern Switzerland, and the Costa Smeralda, on the rugged north-east coast of the island of Sardegna – Sardinia. For my parents, and later for me as well, Lugano was the place they came from, even though the family lived all over the world for long stretches at a time. Lugano was where I was born, married, lived and have visited frequently since. The language at home was Italian, our food was northern Italian and the centre of our mental landscape was that area between the Alps and the great city of the Lombard Plains, Milano. Sardegna was where we spent our summers, at a white-washed Mediterranean house, looking out over a changing sea to the islands of the Maddalena archipelago and beyond them to the towering distant peaks of Corsica.

When you move from places, memory plays some tricks. The colours seem sharper, the people take on slightly mythical proportions and the life you lived there is bathed in golden light. I have lived much of my life away from Lugano, firstly for eight years in Iran, then at school in Zurich and later, after travelling the world for years, in Sydney, Australia. But I have always returned to Lugano and the Costa Smeralda as often as I can to see my family and to immerse myself in the life there.

I am a passionate amateur cook so food plays an important part in this story. I love growing it, buying it, preparing it, serving it and, of course, the rituals of cooking it. Food is at the centre of our family life. Above all, the moment when it all comes together for me, when I feel I am creating something magical, is when we enjoy simple food in an outdoor setting. At such times the ingredients seem to blend and create something that, like the truly memorable dishes of the world, is greater than the sum of their parts.

It is what I call al fresco living – and it is, by far and away, my favourite way to eat. Just what makes al fresco living and the food that goes with it will be different for everyone: it is very much a personal thing. To me it means to be uncomplicated and relaxed, the opposite of everything that is stiff, formal, stuffy or over-elaborate. It begins with an attitude of mind as much as anything else. There are no particular rules – the choices, settings and styles are your own.

My own food is a grab bag of styles and influences. It is grounded in the north Italian cooking of my childhood, but has elements from the places where I have lived and the things I have enjoyed wherever I have been, my personal scrapbook of likes and dislikes. There is nothing purist about my food – sometimes I feel that if you could read my lunch table as a book, it would be the story of my life.

Cooking is also in my blood. My great-grandfather founded a restaurant 120 years ago. His son, my grandfather, made it famous and my mother was a renowned home cook. The restaurant was in Lugano, queen city of an alpine lake, so this is where the journey begins. Last year I travelled back there, in summer of course, with photographer Simon Griffiths. Together we have tried to capture the elusive qualities of these places and the life I lived there.

So travel back with me to enjoy what I see, to taste what I taste and perhaps be a little inspired too.

otto Lago di Lugano. Oria.

Lugano
QUEEN CITY OF AN ALPINE *Lake*

Left: View of Lugano inland to Monte Bolia. Above: An old photograph of lakeside Lugano.

THE CITY OF LUGANO SPRAWLS COMFORTABLY BETWEEN THE TWO IMPOSING peaks of Monte San Salvatore and Monte Bre, on an open bend in the middle of the lake that bears its name. Over the hill, at the south end of the lake, is the city of Como and an hour further south from Como, presiding over the Lombardy Plains, is the centre of gravity for the whole area, the city of Milano.

Lugano prides itself on being the sunroom of Switzerland. Many is the train traveller from Zurich who has entered the San Gottardo Tunnel amidst grey skies and emerged on the other side into the sunshine of the south, the Swiss Canton of Ticino. Culturally, Lugano is a good mix of Italian influences in architecture, food and fashion combined with the Swiss genius for making things work. Traditionally, it has been a holiday destination ever since the railway from the north reached the city when the San Gottardo Tunnel opened in 1882. Even now Lugano's population swells in the summer as northerners flock to its balmy climate.

Today, the real secret of Lugano cannot be seen at street level; not, at least, unless you look carefully. Above the colonnades of smart shops are the offices of a vast number of banks. Lugano, outwardly pleasantly small (it has a population of 60,000 people) and provincial, is a money-centre of world-class size and influence.

Below: The village of Gandria clings to the side of the lake. Right: Views of the village of Morcote.

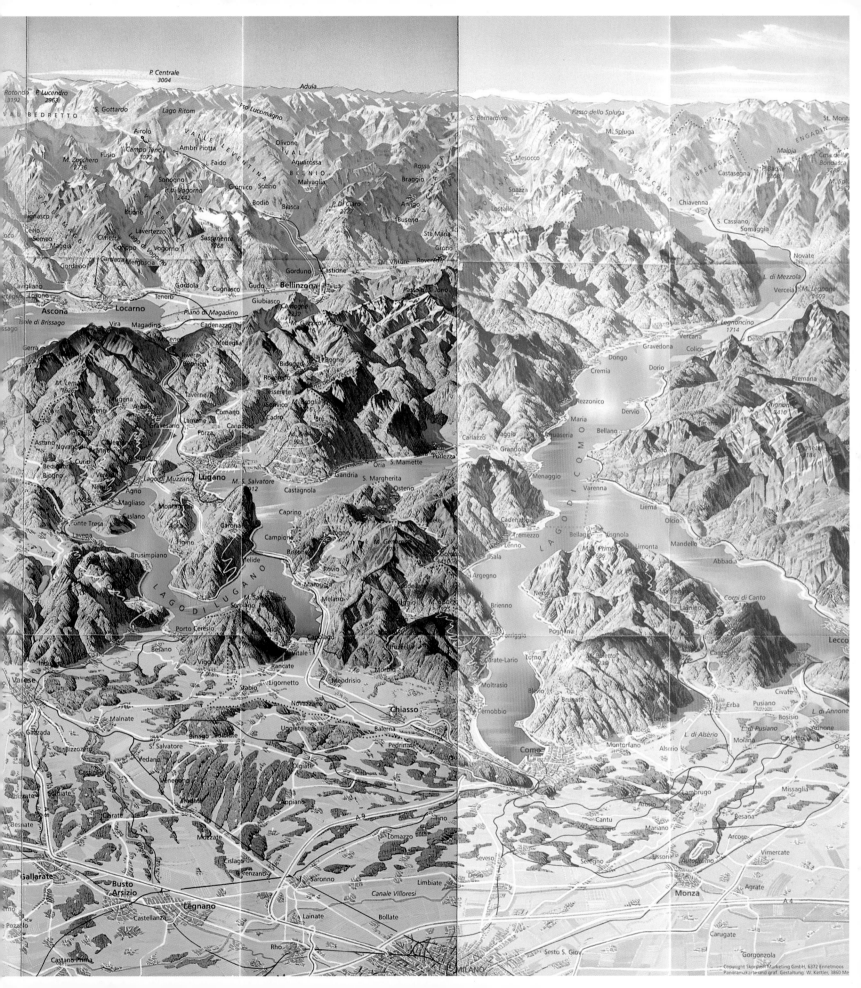

*Top: Kailas.
Above: The old silkworm
building that became
Kailas. This is how it
looked in 1930.*

Most of the industry and wealth of Italy is located along the Torino–Venezia (Turin–Venice) corridor and, ultimately, most of that wealth seems to bank in Lugano. It is not the capital of the Ticino but it is by far the most important city. Little of this is obvious to the casual visitor strolling through the squares but the evidence is everywhere for those with a keen eye – Lugano is a prosperous town.

My family on both my mother's and father's sides were from Lugano. Our home is on a hill on the outskirts of the city, near the village of Rovello, looking down at the lake and across to the two mountains on either side of it. A hundred years ago the area used to be gardens and vineyards; the house itself is very old, and originally housed silkworms. Now we are surrounded by new buildings and most of the gardens on the hillside are gone.

But our house is still set in a leafy oasis. Once you step under the arched gateway of stone and brick, you enter a world of old walls, big spreading trees and a secret garden which still has distant views of lake, mountain and sky.

The house is called 'Kailas' after the renowned holy mountain in Tibet and, from a distance, it does look at bit like a *dzong* – the Tibetan mountain house. My father was a great adventurer and traveller and, as a young man, in the 1930s made a

famous secret trip into Tibet to Mt Kailas alone and disguised as a monk on a pilgrimage to the holy mountain. Today the house is filled with the mementos of his long and active life, much of it spent in the wild places of the world.

Next door, sharing the same garden, lives my brother Luca when he is in Switzerland. Luca is a painter and has roamed all over the world. For the last five years he has lived mainly in Thailand and has been exploring the remote culture of the Moken sea gypsies of the Andaman Sea off Burma. He is in town now to work on an exhibition of paintings at a gallery in Zurich.

Kailas, the house and the garden, has a timeless quality and is a place full of memories for me. My father Augusto, now 93, still lives there and works diligently at his books. A new one, covering some aspect of his long and adventurous life, seems to come out every year. Even when we lived elsewhere we often used to go back to Lugano for holidays, particularly in autumn and spring. It was always at the centre of our family world.

I was born in Lugano, went there often as a child and have lived there or visited most years since then. About a decade ago I returned to live in Lugano for a year and our children went to local schools to learn Italian and to experience being

The façade of my grandfather's restaurant in Lugano. The family lived above the restaurant.

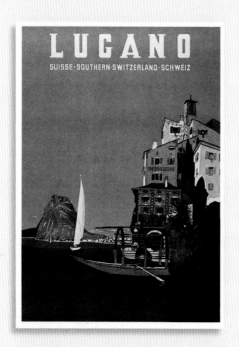

Left: Old postcards
of Lugano.
Right: Lugano's
lakeside promenade.

Luganesi. Earlier, when we only had one child, we lived for a year in Milano and Lugano was then our weekend retreat.

So my sentimental journey starts in Lugano. My father is there, Luca is back from his travels and my other brother, Mario, will be coming down from the north of Switzerland. I want to enjoy again their company, the house, the garden, the lake and the surrounding mountains and valleys.

After arriving by train from Zurich, a timeless journey through the Alps and the traditional way to arrive in Lugano, we decide to eat out at a simple trattoria on a hillside near the station, with a commanding view of the lake. It is called 'Il Trenin', a local dialect word meaning 'the little train', and is a favourite of my father. The evening is warm and still and pinpoints of lights are spread out below us like a magic carpet. You see what you want to see and I see only the Old Lugano of my childhood. Two lines of lights rise up, one to the top of Monte Bre and the other to the top of Monte San Salvatore. They mark the pathways of the steep funicular railways to their summits, but from where we sit they look like stairways to the stars.

For that first evening I want to eat something typical of the place, something that will make me feel I have really arrived.

My dinner starts with a local soup, Zuppa alle Ortiche, made from nettles – a classic example of the 'cucina povera', or poor people's cooking, that I like so much. Today nettles can be found in the produce markets, but of course in the old days they were gathered wild. Don't worry about the sting – once nettles are cooked they lose it. What you get is a subtle, almost nutty flavour which makes an unusual and very satisfying soup.

To follow, I choose Ucelli Scappati – literally 'flown-away birds'. Originally this was made with small birds cooked on a skewer and eaten whole, bones and all. Now the birds are left to sing in peace and a mix of veal, calves liver and bacon is grilled on the skewer. The fine flavour of the veal contrasting with the stronger liver and bacon gives a slightly gamey flavour to the dish, perhaps reminiscent of the original birds.

The dish is served with that most traditional of accompaniments in the Ticino – polenta. Ever since maize was imported into Europe from the New World the rich plains at the base of the Alps have been one of the main centres of its cultivation. For a long time now polenta has been a staple food for the people of southern Switzerland; in the past it was often eaten three times a day. For breakfast it was served with milk and cream, for lunch with cheese or vegetables and in the evening with meat stews or with mushrooms.

The local architecture evolved to meet the needs of maize cultivation, with the top floor of village houses often being built as an open granary to store the corn.

Even today you can see some old houses with festoons of corn under high eaves, giving an air of promise and plenty to carry them through the hard winter. So to eat polenta on my first night in Lugano is to taste the essence of the city.

Finally, to clear the palate, I have a marvellous bitter sorbet made from grapefruit – ideally it should be pink grapefruit for its colour – mixed with Campari. The twin bitter tastes of grapefruit and Campari are an unusual and bracing combination – and the colour is extraordinary.

To accompany this dinner, we drink the local red wine made, like most wines in Ticino, from merlot grapes, known there as 'uva americana', American grapes. It is made from vines that seem to cling for life to the south-facing slopes of hillsides everywhere locally. They are not hugely distinguished wines, but they are well made, have a local resonance and match the food very well. That evening we drank a wine called La Montana Magica, which translates as 'The Magic Mountain', a soft and full wine from the Malcantone Valley. It is a romantic name for a wine, but this was rather a romantic evening.

Far left, from top to bottom: View down Lake Lugano towards Italy; Papa in the garden at Kailas; Coffee in the garden. Above: Lugano – city architecture.

13

Zuppa ALLE *Ortiche*

NETTLE SOUP

600 g (1 lb 5 oz) fresh nettles

1 large Spanish onion, chopped

1 medium leek, chopped

25 g (1 oz) butter and
2 tablespoons olive oil

2.5 litres (5 pints) fresh chicken
or vegetable stock

1 chilli (optional)

2 egg yolks

about 2 handfuls freshly grated
parmigiano cheese, or to taste

freshly ground black pepper

*Put gloves on when preparing nettles. Use only leaves
and fine stalks of the plant, discarding the thick stems.*
Fry onion and leek in a mix of butter and olive oil.
When soft add the nettles and stir quickly for a few
seconds, then add the stock and chilli. Boil for about
3–4 minutes then remove from heat.

In a small bowl beat egg yolks with a fork, add a
ladleful of soup to egg yolks, stir in and then mix this
back into rest of soup. Do not let the soup boil again.
Add parmigiano and some pepper.

Serve with extra parmigiano on the side.

Variation

*If you like, you can grill 2–3 slices of ciabatta bread or
firm white bread, sprinkle them with some olive oil, then
cut into small squares and at the last minute add these
'crostini' to the soup.*

Serves 6

Polenta

2–2.5 litres (4–5 pints) water

2 teaspoons sea salt

500 g (1 lb 2 oz) polenta
(corn meal)

This is the basic recipe.

Bring water and salt to the boil in a large pot. Add the polenta in a steady stream, whisking constantly so as not to form lumps.

Turn the heat right down and then stir well with a wooden spoon. Be careful as the hot polenta will 'pop' like a volcano and you could burn yourself.

Let the polenta cook for about 45 minutes, stirring very often. In the last 5 minutes of cooking do not stir any more, just shake the pot. The polenta should come away easily from the sides – that is the sign it is ready.

Polenta is traditionally served by pouring it on to a dampened wooden board and then cutting it with a wooden polenta knife or with string. You can also dampen a clean tea towel and put it in a flat basket, then pour the polenta into it.

Serves 6–8

Ucelli *Scappati*

FLOWN-AWAY BIRDS

300 g (10½oz) calves liver,
sliced about 2 cm (¾in) thick

300 g (10½ oz) veal nut (noix,
or topside), sliced about
2 cm (¾ in) thick

150 g (5 oz) pancetta,
sliced ½ cm (¼ in) thick

plain (all-purpose) flour

fresh sage leaves

2–3 cloves garlic, chopped

300 ml (10 fl oz) dry white wine

salt and pepper

Cut the liver, veal and pancetta into cubes.
Flour the liver and veal. Then, alternating,
thread the liver, sage, veal and pancetta on skewers.
Take a pan large enough to hold all the skewers at
once and in a bit of butter and oil, brown the skewers
of meat one or two at a time on all sides, then set
aside on a dish.
Add the garlic to the pan with a few more sage leaves.
Let the garlic become golden (do not burn it) then
add the wine and scrape all the bits in the bottom
of the pan. When it bubbles add the skewers, salt
and pepper and let them cook, covered, for about
20 minutes on low heat.
If it seems too dry before cooking is finished
add a bit of veal or chicken stock.

Serves 6

Sorbetto

DI POMPELMO ROSA CON *Campari*

PINK GRAPEFRUIT AND CAMPARI SORBET

4–5 large pink grapefruits, juiced

120 g (4 oz) caster (superfine) sugar

½ cup Campari

5 drops Angostura bitters

Mix all ingredients well. When sugar has dissolved, put in ice-cream machine and churn until fluffy and light coloured.

Spoon the sorbet into glasses and finish off with a little bit more Campari on top. The sorbet should not be too sweet.

Serves 6–8

Menu

Mettere al sole il vaso
colle noci – aggiungere
quindi gli ingredienti
e riesporre per altri
15 giorni.

1911

Cooking
IS IN MY *Blood*

MY GRANDFATHER, ETTORE BIAGGI, KNOWN TO US AS NONNINO, HAD A famous restaurant in Lugano called, appropriately, Ristorante Biaggi. It had been founded by his father in 1882, the year the railway line from the north reached Lugano. One of Nonnino's two daughters, my aunt Zia Bruna, had a hotel in Lugano and her husband, Zio Camillo, was a talented and creative professional chef from whom I learned to cook pizza and other dishes. Nonnino's other daughter, my mother, Toti Gansser-Biaggi, was an inspired home cook.

Ristorante Biaggi was in Via Pessina, about one block from the main square, Piazza Riforma, and right next to the famous shopping colonnades of Via Nassa, which stretch for a kilometre. Then, as now, there were specialist food shops in the Via Pessina selling breads, cheeses, fruit, vegetables and local wine. My mother grew up living over the restaurant. Despite being surrounded by the day-to-day business of food preparation, she did not learn to cook as a child because all the family's meals came from the restaurant's kitchen. When she became engaged to my father, she asked the chef, Julio Casella, to teach her the basics of culinary survival in a very short time. He was so painfully shy that, instead, Nonnino had to write out his recipes in an exercise book, which I still have. Something must have rubbed off,

Left: Ettore and Clelia Biaggi with their two children, my Zio Bubi and Zia Bruna. Mamma came later.
Above: Nonnino in the garden at Kailas.

however, because my mother became a wonderful cook, who throughout her long life was always trying new dishes and delighting us with the results. She inherited her father's creativity and love of food and placed it at the centre of our family life.

Ettore Biaggi ran a very successful restaurant. As a young man, he trained in grand hotels in London, Paris and St Petersburg. He took a small family restaurant and made it famous. The guest book of the restaurant was known as the Libro d'Oro, the golden book. In it you can see a procession of names of the great, good and notorious of the day – the Aga Khan, Sir Austen Chamberlain, Mussolini, General Guissan, Dolfuss, Mannerheim and King Farouk of Egypt.

A family story has it that the wife of Austen Chamberlain, the British Foreign Secretary at the time, was visiting the restaurant with her husband who was engaged in a round of peace-making at a conference in Locarno on nearby Lago Maggiore. Lady Chamberlain was so enamoured of the zabaglione semifreddo that she marched into the kitchen to get the chef, the same shy Julio, to teach her then and there how to make it. Julio went into shock when told later who the great lady was.

Ettore Biaggi was also one of the first of what we now know as celebrity chefs. The new medium was the radio and he had a cooking program every Wednesday

Top: Family Christmas at Kailas in 1957. Mamma is on the far right next to Papa. I am next to him.
Above: Mamma's book of Nonnino's recipes.

A festive dinner at Ristorante Biaggi, upstairs in Il Cenacolo.

afternoon. He was known as 'Cuoco delle Onde' or 'cook of the airwaves'. During World War II, his program developed a more serious purpose as he tried to create recipes that could be cooked with the limited ingredients available in a time of austerity. From cooking with the best ingredients, often rare and costly, he now had to make do with the basics. It was what Italians call cucina povera.

Ironically, much of what we cook and eat today is closer to cucina povera than it is to the grand old cuisine of the nineteenth century. Polenta, risotto, pasta and pizza are the classic descendants of cucina povera. Their simplicity and lightness are right for today's living and I regularly use a number of these wartime recipes today. Two creations in particular, Pâté di Tonno (tuna fish pâté) and Risotto di Pasta, I have included here in memory of my grandfather and as a tribute to his creativity. They are as good now as when he first devised them.

Nonnino was a passionately creative man. He filled his restaurant and his life with the things he loved. Fresh flowers came in every day from his abundant and renowned garden in the village of Rovello, just a little up the hill from Kailas. He bought beautiful furniture, which he could not always afford, and filled the restaurant with special plates, silverware and glasses. Today in the house we still

have some of those plates that were made for the restaurant; on them are entwined his initials with those of his wife Clelia.

He also created a special banqueting room on the first floor of the restaurant. It was decorated in the traditional Florentine manner by an Italian artist, Buonafede, and was known as 'Il Cenacolo'. This room quickly became a famous meeting place in Lugano and could be used for theatre and music as well as dining. During World War II, it was also a clandestine meeting place for Italian partisans. We still drink on special occasions from the octagonal wine glasses made for Il Cenacolo on the island of Murano in the Venice Lagoon.

Much of the garden at Kailas was also Nonnino's work, as he renovated the house and established the garden while my parents were living in Colombia, South America. He turned a run-down old agricultural building into a family house of simple elegance and charm, so his spirit lives on in that house and its garden.

My mother absorbed this passion and creativity from her father, together with a certain level-headedness from her mother. And I learned what I know from my mother. From her I got the urge to keep learning, keep experimenting and keep creating. She was the great influence on my food, as she was on my whole life.

So you see, we have had serious cooks in the family for 120 years and cooking is in my blood. I probably could not escape it if I wanted to – which I certainly do not.

I have included here three of Nonnino's recipes: two from his cucina povera wartime period and, in a grand contrast, Lady Chamberlain's zabaglione semifreddo. Full of rich and subtle flavours, I think you will see, if you try it, why she was so enthusiastic about this dish.

Pâté di Tonno was devised as an alternative to more traditional pâtés of the time, made with goose or duck livers and often finished with truffles. These rich ingredients were not available during the war so Nonnino created for his listeners this dish, made from the simplest of basic ingredients – tinned tuna. The recipe in the book is slightly different from his – some in my family think it is secret and can't be passed on so I have altered it slightly. But this is the recipe I use when I make Paté di Tonno.

Risotto di Pasta he created because rice, the beautiful arborio rice needed for risotto, was not often available at the time as it came from Italy, then at war. In this dish, conciglie, the shell-shaped pasta, is cooked in the same broth you would use for risotto. The broth is not absorbed, as it is by the rice in a risotto, but flavours the pasta. When you take a spoonful of pasta, a little of the broth will be in every shell, which is why the shape of the pasta is so important. It is a dish of inspired simplicity and is quite delicious.

L'oratorio di San Rocco prima dei restauri

Pâté

DI *Tonno*

TUNA FISH PÂTÉ

150 g (5 oz) unsalted butter

1 large Spanish onion, chopped

1 large shallot, chopped

400 g (14 oz) canned tuna in oil

1 bay leaf

2 sprigs fresh tarragon, finely chopped

10 anchovy fillets, chopped finely

½ cup Oloroso sherry

freshly ground black pepper

Use about 50 g (2 oz) of butter and cook onion and shallot until soft and transparent. Add herbs and anchovies. After a few minutes add the sherry and let it evaporate. Add the remaining butter, cut into pieces, and let it melt gently, making sure it does not bubble.

Put the drained tuna and the butter mixture into a food processor, removing the bay leaf. Mix well (for about 5–10 minutes) until mixture becomes a very pale colour.

Taste for seasoning and add pepper if necessary. Pour into a bowl and leave in refrigerator until it becomes hard.

Variation

You can add 1–2 large boiled, mashed potatoes to the pâté to make it go further or lighten the taste.

Serves 6

Risotto
DI *Pasta*
RISOTTO OF PASTA

1 large red Spanish onion

**500 g (1 lb 2 oz)
shell-shaped pasta**

**1 glass (about 200 ml / 7 fl oz)
dry white wine**

**2–2.5 litres (4–5 pints) fresh,
strong chicken stock**

1 tablespoon unsalted butter

**2 tablespoons freshly grated
parmigiano cheese**

Chop the onion and heat in a bit of butter and olive oil, until it has softened. Now pour in the pasta and let it cook for 2–3 minutes, stirring well. Add the glass of wine and let it evaporate.

Add half the stock, bring to the boil and continue to cook, stirring occasionally. If it gets too dry add more stock. Pasta should still be al dente when it is ready – about 8–10 minutes. Take off stove, add unsalted butter and parmigiano and stir well. Serve immediately. The pasta should be quite moist.

Have more parmigiano on the side at table.

Serves 4

Semifreddo

DI Zabaglione
ZABAGLIONE SEMIFREDDO

6 organic eggs, separated

110 g (4 oz) caster
(superfine) sugar

150 ml (5 fl oz) good marsala

500 ml (1 pint) whipped cream

Beat egg yolks and sugar together until light, then add marsala and beat again until light and fluffy.

Put bowl over a double boiler, allow water in lower pan to simmer, and whisk mixture until it increases in volume and becomes like a thick cream. Set aside and let it cool.

Beat the egg whites until stiff but not dry. Mix the whipped cream with the egg yolk, sugar and marsala mixture then fold in the egg whites.

Pour into a square dish, cover and put in freezer for at least 6 hours.

Scoop the ice cream out and put into glasses. The ice cream should still be a little bit soft – 'semifreddo' means 'half-frozen'.

Serves 8

La Cucina
DELLA *Mamma*

Above: Breakfast on the verandah in Tehran with Mamma, Ursula, Mario and Luca. I am the little one on the right.

I THINK EVERYONE WHO HAS A PASSION FOR FOOD HAS PROBABLY HAD someone who triggered that interest and helped to encourage it. For me that person was my mother, Toti Gansser-Biaggi; for her it was her father. Nonnino died when I was only eight years old so I grew up with the stories of his life, but was too young to be influenced by him directly.

My mother had an adventurous life living all over the world and managed at the same time to raise six children. As a teenager she was a champion backstroke swimmer, practising, in those days before heated swimming pools, in the cold waters of Lake Lugano off the Lido beach. When she married my father her adventures began. A honeymoon spent in a tent touring the hinterland of Morocco was a taste of things to come. She then spent eight years living in the high Andean city of Bogota in Colombia. In the early years of her marriage, she often accompanied my father on his expeditions in the mountains, sometimes travelling for months at a time. One lasting result of these travels is an Andean mountain peak that is named after her – Piz Toti.

The family then moved to Venezuela, on to Trinidad and finally, after I was born, to Tehran where I spent the first eight years of my life. They say that a child's life is formed by those first early years and for me it is true. My memories of life in Iran are still vivid: I lived in an earthly paradise – a beautiful garden on the outskirts of Tehran with water, flowers and fruit trees, all surrounded by high walls.

We had our animals – a donkey, deer, cats and dogs, geese, ducks and hens. This whole world was guided and ordered by the powerful and benevolent figure of La Mamma.

Outside the walls all was different – bustling, crowded, exciting, even on a few occasions dangerous. On one side were some open fields, and every few weeks or so a caravan of camels would arrive and camp there. My favourite day was market day, which happened two or three times a week. Our helper, Ali, and Mamma and I would head off to the nearby market. It was a heady world of dealing, masses of people and the aroma of fresh and dried spices. One shop would sell live chickens (their heads would be chopped off on purchase, leaving the poor headless bird to fly briefly through the air); another would have different types of rice, lentils, pistachios, raisins and almonds. The vegetable and fruit shops would have apricots that dreams are made of, cherries, mulberries, figs and my favourite, pomegranate, with its ruby-red seeds and dark red juice that we would drink fresh every morning. I suppose my love of produce markets has come from my experiences in the markets of Tehran: for me markets are an indispensable part of the world of food.

As a child you are not aware your life is special in any way – you just think this is how the world is. It is only later that it takes on rather mythological proportions. We camped on the beach on the shores of the Caspian Sea. We trudged up mountain slopes outside Tehran to get a short ski run down. I have memories of roller-skating around the Golestan Palace in Tehran with my friend Dodi, who was the daughter of Princess Ashraf, the Shah's twin sister.

At the centre of this life was my mother and the centre of her world was the courtyard garden of the house in Tehran. There on warm evenings the garden would be spread with rugs and cushions, lanterns would gleam and flicker and she would prepare food that we would help take around on large plates and platters, to be eaten casually at low tables. She adapted the North Italian cooking of her childhood to her new circumstances and readily sought out Iranian dishes to add to her repertoire. What she did, in effect, was to create her own style of al fresco eating well before it became understood and accepted, as it is now. In that sense she was a pioneer.

So you can imagine the influence my memories of this time have on me. When I smell jasmine or pomegranate my childhood in Iran comes flooding back. In a way the memories of that time probably still guide me, as I unconsciously seek to create for my own family and friends the world of that paradise garden that Mamma created for us.

It was a terrible shock to my system when at the age of nine all this life ended and we moved to the bracing northern climate of Zurich. Not even Zurich's most enthusiastic supporters would describe the city, for all its merits, as exotic and colourful. It was the opposite of the life I had led until then.

My mother still worked hard to keep the dream alive. At her parties she would serve casual al fresco food and the house was full of beautiful carpets and objects from Iran and South America. Food was still an important ritual in the house, not only eating together but also helping to 'chop this' or 'stir that' in the small kitchen which was really the heart of the house. While the food preparation was going there would be a stream of talk, questions and advice on the lives of her various children. Her kitchen was a place of comfort and warmth and, for her, a place where she demonstrated through food her love for us all.

In Zurich it was harder to live the al fresco life – the climate was very much against it! But we did try. I can remember numerous occasions when a weak winter sun would appear for a moment at midday and my father would call for coffee on the terrace even as the snow lay on the ground.

Of course this made our trips to Lugano, the warm sunny south, all the more welcome. There we could begin to live again the life of the paradise garden.

I am including here four recipes from our time in Iran. Two are rice dishes, Polo (which means rice in the Iranian language, Farsi) ba Sumac and Addas Polo ba Bareh.

Polo ba Sumac is a simple but unusual dish made by breaking and mixing raw eggs with cooked rice. The unusual element is sumac, an astringent spice; its red-brown granules are made from the ground small berries of the sumac bush. Sumac is sprinkled over the rice and provides colour and an exotic flavour. It is also used in Iran sprinkled over grilled meats.

Addas Polo ba Bareh is a dish made with rice, lentils and lamb – classic ingredients of Iranian cooking.

The other two recipes are for Cumquats in Brandy and Cherries in Brandy. Mamma would make them from the fruit that grew in abundance in our garden and I remember well the line of jars filled with cumquats or cherries that would sit on a shelf in the kitchen of the house in Tehran. The scent of these drinks today overwhelmingly reminds me of that magic time.

We still use the old Iranian silver samovar for tea at Kailas.

Polo

BA Sumac

RICE WITH SUMAC

500 g (1 lb 2 oz) basmati
or long-grain rice

100 g (3½ oz) unsalted butter

sumac (see Note)

8–12 eggs

*In Iran lamb kebabs are often served with this polo.
The lamb is cut into cubes, marinated in lemon juice, oil
and finely chopped onions, threaded on to narrow skewers
and grilled over charcoal. The whole dish, kebab and
polo, is then called 'Chelo Kebab'.*

Rinse rice several times in cold water. Add rice to
about 2 litres (4 pints) boiling, salted water and cook
until still a little al dente. Strain quickly.

In a pan melt butter, put rice in pan and toss gently.
Then pile rice on a warmed dish and sprinkle some
sumac over it.

Calculating 2 egg yolks per person, carefully separate
the eggs, discarding the whites and keeping the yolks
in their shells. Stand shells in a shallow dish filled
with salt: the salt should be deep enough to hold the
eggshells upright.

Serve the rice and yolks at the table. Put some rice
on your plate, add the 2 raw egg yolks, then sprinkle
some more sumac over them. Mix and eat.

Note

*Sumac is a souring agent; it is a red-brown powder made
from the dried ground berries of the sumac bush. You can
buy sumac in Middle Eastern shops. It is also sprinkled
on lamb kebabs and stews.*

Serves 4–6

Addas
POLO BA *Bareh*

SPICED LAMB AND RICE

500 g (1 lb 2 oz) basmati
or long-grain rice

1½ cups small brown lentils

1½ teaspoons salt

1 egg yolk

¾ cup thick plain yoghurt

½ cup melted butter

250 g (9 oz) lamb fillet,
chopped in small pieces

1 red onion, chopped

2 cloves garlic, chopped

1 teaspoon ground turmeric

2 teaspoons ground cumin

1 teaspoon ground cinnamon

½ teaspoon ground nutmeg

Rinse rice well in cold water 2–3 times. Bring 2 litres
(4 pints) salted water to the boil, add rice and parboil
the rice – about 5 minutes – and strain.

Cover lentils with cold water, add salt and bring to
the boil. Cook for about 20 minutes. The lentils
should still be a little al dente. Drain and set aside.

Mix 1½ cups of the rice with the egg yolk, yoghurt
and melted butter. Put this in a non-stick, buttered
heavy pan, and set aside.

In another pan, melt a little butter and cook lamb,
onion and garlic until lamb has browned and onion
softened – about 5 minutes. Add spices.

Now mix the remaining parboiled plain rice and the
lentils with the lamb mixture and pile it on top of
the yoghurt and rice mixture. With a wooden spoon
handle, make holes in the rice and add some small
pieces of butter. Put the lid on tight and, over a
very low heat, cook for about 30–40 minutes.

To serve, turn it upside down on to a warm dish.
The rice should have a beautiful golden crust on top.

Serves 8

Cherries IN *Brandy*

1 kg (2 lb 3 oz) ripe, dark and firm cherries (leave stalks on)

500 g (1 lb 2 oz) sugar

700 ml (1½ pints) good brandy

1 cinnamon stick

3 cloves

This is fantastic liqueur for after dinner. The fruit can be eaten as well, together with some ice-cream or a panna cotta.

Mix all together and place in a large, sterilised jar. Put in sun for 30 days, shaking the jar each day, then in a dark place for another six months.

Cumquats IN *Brandy*

1 kg (2 lb 3 oz) very firm cumquats

300 g (10½ oz) sugar

1 vanilla bean

700 ml (1½ pints) brandy

This is fantastic liqueur for after dinner. The fruit can be eaten as well, together with some ice-cream or a panna cotta.

Quickly blanch the cumquats in boiling water and drain. Allow to cool and dry well.

With a toothpick prick little holes in the fruit. Put in a large, airtight sterilised jar. Add sugar, vanilla bean and brandy. Put in a dark room, shaking the jar every day until the sugar is well dissolved.

Leave for at least three months.

Under
THE
Olive Tree

IN THE GARDEN AT KAILAS IS AN OLD OLIVE TREE. IT SHADES AND FRAMES A small terrace bounded by a low wall, which drops on its outer side some 4 metres to the road below. From this terrace, which is close to the house, you get the best view of the lake and the mountains beyond. So this is where the outside table and chairs, shaded by the olive tree, are placed and where we eat whenever possible in the summer months. This simple setting is the centre of the world of my memories and imagination.

Behind the terrace is the old wall of the house and high up on the wall is a painted sundial. Apart from the gap that frames the view of the lake and the mountain peaks, one is surrounded by the shrubs, trees and stone walls of the garden. At the end of the garden is the head of an old stone well. It is an enchanted spot – a secret oasis of calm.

On my first day back in Lugano, the sun is out and echoes of the warmth to come are already evident so, naturally, I have breakfast under the olive. I am a light eater at breakfast – usually just coffee and nothing more. We plan the day and decide to have lunch and dinner at the house as various visitors will be dropping by. This means a trip into Lugano to the shops and stalls of the food markets to buy all the

Left: Kailas, the garden and the olive tree.
Above: Swinging the salad to dry it in the garden.

43

*Food on display
in Via Pessina.*

necessary ingredients. It is something I look forward to with pleasure; the process of seeing and choosing the food is very much part of the satisfaction to be had from the lunch or dinner itself.

Today, we decide to walk into Lugano down the winding, cobbled, car-free road to the town centre and take the funicular cable car back up. Immediately below the railway station there are large and rather grand nineteenth-century buildings, apartments and hotels. As we go further into the town the buildings get a little smaller and a little older. We pass the beautiful old façade of the cathedral and pause to admire the panorama from the terrace in front, before heading off down a long steep, stepped road which finishes in a small square surrounded by elegantly restored old town houses (now mostly banks).

This is the beginning of Via Pessina, where all the food shops are, their wares displayed prominently in stalls in front of the shops themselves. Further down the street is the Ristorante Biaggi and I can imagine Nonnino in the midst of all this abundance. In his day, local suppliers came to a courtyard at the rear of the restaurant to display their produce for his selection. Some took home the

'carobbia', or cooked food that the restaurant had prepared but did not need, as during the hard times of the 1930s Nonnino ran his own private soup kitchen. It is nice to speculate that it was because of him this became known as a food area and that these shops I now enjoy have sprung up in response to something that he began.

For a short section Via Pessina is all food shops – on one side the raw materials, on the other some of the most delicious takeaway food from grand delicatessens. The ever-present jewellery, watch and designer clothing shops are banished to either end. Just past the Ristorante Biaggi, whose elegant façade remains but is now trading as a tea room under another name, the street joins a small square with a simple granite basin fed by a spout of pure cold water. Via Pessina was the centre of my mother's childhood world and it still means something special to me.

Just beyond the Via Pessina is the main square of Lugano, the Piazza Riforma, a large paved open space surrounded by handsome buildings on three sides and the imposing façade of the Municipio, or Town Hall, on the fourth. At ground level there are a number of cafés in the square and they spill out under awnings with their tables and chairs. Apart from the cafés and Town Hall the square is wall-to-wall

*Above: Lunch under
the olive tree.
Right: The same table
set for dinner, with the
Murano glasses and
initialled plates from
Ristorante Biaggi.*

banks. Discreetly, elegantly, but very definitely there is the hush of money. Not retail money with ground-floor banking chambers for ordinary people, but large amounts of money managed with great diligence in investments far and wide: what is called in that world 'serious money'.

Money is not on our minds, however, as we head for the square for a coffee before our food shopping. 'Our' bar is the Piccolo Federale (I don't really know why but we have always gone there) and we enjoy an excellent cappuccino while gazing idly at the passers-by in the piazza. The bar also has excellent light food. It was a family tradition, when our children were at school in Lugano, to have a pizza at the Piccolo Federale at lunchtimes on Wednesdays when the local schools have their afternoon off.

Back in Via Pessina I assemble all the ingredients for the coming lunch and dinner. There are two excellent fruit and vegetable shops. At one I buy some mixed salad leaves and select from 12 varieties of tomatoes. At the other I choose raspberries, wild tiny blueberries, wild baby wood strawberries and, the surprise find of the day, fresh porcini mushrooms, their exotic and subtle aroma faintly wafting in the air.

Between the two vegetable stalls are shops selling cheese, bread and local wine. I suppose you would expect that in Switzerland the cheese shops would be exceptional and here you would not be disappointed. I am after the local cheeses from the Ticino valleys made from cows' milk or a mix of cows' and sheep's milk. The proprietor knows his cheeses and is able to point out which valley they come from and whether it is 'this year's cheese, last year's, or the year before that'. I make my selection, one more tempting than the next, and head to the bread shop next door.

It may be a little known fact, but the bread shops of Switzerland are very much the equal of the cheese shops and, to my mind, superior to what you usually find in Italy. Swiss bakeries stock all the Italian-style breads — such as the ciabatta and focaccia — but you also see an enormous range of crusty, rich, darker breads ranging from light to dark brown, which are a triumph of breadmaking and are particularly good when accompanying Swiss cheeses. After filling my basket with a selection of breads, we stop at the wine shop for some local merlot which they will deliver. My final purchase is a beautiful organic chicken from the delicatessen, and then it is off to the funicular station and home.

For lunch I have in mind to serve the cheeses and breads and to use the selection of salads to make a Pollo Capriccioso (literally 'capricious chicken') which is cold chicken on a riot of salad leaves and raw vegetables and served with a very lemony mayonnaise. It looks sensational on a large white platter, and it tastes as good as it looks.

Dinner under the olive tree with Michele, Gabi, Luca and Papa.

For dinner I will make a classic dish from this area – Risotto alla Milanese made with fresh broth from the leftover chicken and served with fresh porcini mushrooms. It could not be simpler but, like all simple dishes, it has to be just right or it will be very obviously wrong. To follow will be the Frutti di Bosco, or wild fruits of the woods – the raspberries, wild strawberries and blueberries, simply topped with lemon and caster sugar.

Later that night, as we sit outside under the olive tree, washed with the warm night air and gazing out over the lights of Lugano across the silver of the lake to the blackness of the steep mountainsides beyond, I am filled with contentment. With my family around me it is, as the Italian saying goes, 'A tavola non si invecchia' – at the table you don't grow old.

Funghi *Porcini*

PORCINI MUSHROOMS

3-4 fresh porcini mushrooms
or 2 packets of dried ones

1-2 cloves of garlic, chopped

1 tablespoon butter

flour for dusting

250 ml (8½ fl oz)
dry white wine

Maldon sea salt and freshly
ground black pepper, to taste

handful of flat-leaved Italian
parsley, chopped

There is no substitute for porcini. However, if fresh are not available you can buy dried porcini which need to be soaked before use.

The mushrooms must be very firm to the touch, with no holes in the stalks. Slice them lengthways, so as to have stem and cap together.

Chop the garlic and fry it in the butter but do not let it go brown.

Dust the mushrooms very lightly with flour. Add them to the garlic and mix well. When they start to soften slightly, add about 1 glass dry white wine. Mix well and quickly, being careful not to break the mushrooms. Add salt and pepper and flat-leaved Italian parsley.

The porcini should only take about 5 minutes to cook.

Serves 4–6 as a side dish

Pollo *Capriccioso*

CAPRICIOUS CHICKEN

5 organic chicken breasts

1 red capsicum (bell pepper)

1 yellow capsicum (bell pepper)

2–3 celery sticks

2–3 carrots

iceberg lettuce or radicchio
(red chicory) leaves

Maldon salt and freshly
ground black pepper

2½ cups home-made
mayonnaise (see page 62),
made very lemony

arugula (rocket) leaves

½ cup toasted pine nuts

MARINADE

½ cup virgin olive oil

½ cup lemon juice

2–3 cloves garlic, chopped

1 chilli, chopped

2–3 bay leaves, chopped

Mix together all marinade ingredients and marinate chicken breasts for about 30 minutes.

Preheat the oven to 200°C (400°F). Heat a large cast-iron griddle or pan, add a little olive oil to it and then sear the breasts to brown them, then finish off in the oven for about 20 minutes, or until done. Let them cool, then cut into 2 cm (½ in) strips. Season with salt and pepper.

Cut all the vegetables into thin julienne.

Arrange on your serving dish some baby iceberg or radicchio leaves. Mix the carrots and celery in ½ cup of mayonnaise. Place on to the leaves then add the capsicums, followed by the chicken pieces. Put a handful of arugula leaves on top of chicken and, lastly, scatter over the pine nuts.

Serve the remainder of the mayonnaise on the side.

Serves 6

Risotto
ALLA *Milanese*
MILANESE RISOTTO

approx. 2 litres (4 pints)
well-flavoured fresh
chicken or veal stock

1 large yellow onion, chopped

50 g (2 oz) butter and
3 tablespoons olive oil

bone marrow
(optional, see Note)

pinch of saffron

1 kg (2 lb 3 oz) carnaroli
or arborio rice

300 ml (10 fl oz) dry white wine

80 g (3 oz) unsalted butter

freshly grated parmigiano

salt and pepper

Allow the stock to come to the boil and then turn heat down and simmer.

In a large, heavy-based pot fry the onion in butter and oil until transparent, then add the bone marrow and mix quickly. Add the saffron and then the rice.

Coat rice well with the oil, butter and marrow mix. Let it toast for 1–2 minutes then add the wine, stirring vigorously until it has evaporated.

Add about half the stock to the rice and stir continuously over high heat. When the rice gets a bit dry, add more stock, this time one ladle at a time (the more stock you use the more flavour the risotto will have). After about 20 minutes the rice should be ready. It should still be a bit al dente.

Turn off the heat off and add butter and 1 cup grated parmigiano. Taste for salt, add if needed, and add pepper. Serve immediately with more parmigiano on the side: risotto can't wait!

Note

Ask the butcher to cut 2 large veal bones lengthways, so you will be able to remove the marrow. The marrow is optional in this recipe, but it does make the risotto taste fantastic.

Serves 6–8

Frutti DI *Bosco*

FRUITS OF THE WOODS

1 punnet strawberries

1 punnet blueberries

1 punnet raspberries

juice of 1 lemon, mixed with 2–3 tablespoons caster (superfine) sugar

For best results, use small wild strawberries, if you can find them.

Hull strawberries and let them marinate in the lemon and sugar for about 20 minutes. Just before serving, add the other berries.

Serves 6

Franco's
GREEN HARVEST FOR A
Summer Night

FRANCO SERENA IS AN OLD FRIEND OF MY BROTHER LUCA'S. FOR SOME YEARS now we have been going to his restaurant which is in a plain, rather solid nineteenth-century town house of two storeys set in a garden with spreading old trees. It is not far from Kailas, up through the village of San Rocco – where I was married in a small chapel on a hill surrounded by chestnut woods nearly 30 years ago.

Although it is a little way out of Lugano, Franco's is popular partly because he has a well-deserved reputation for his food, but also because the restaurant is not far from the headquarters of RTV Ticino, the local radio and TV broadcasting corporation. Particularly at lunchtime you are likely to find the media crowd, mixed with other appreciative diners, enjoying the pleasures of his cooking. Perhaps because of this, Franco has also appeared on Ticino TV cooking shows and is well known in the area.

The day we are to have dinner there, Franco asks us to his house nearby to see his famous organic vegetable garden, which is the main source of salads and vegetables for the restaurant. The house is a short drive up a well-hidden gravel road, which winds to a beautiful old Ticinese villa rambling in an old garden with spreading trees. There are ducks, young children and friendly dogs all running

Left: Franco Serena on the stairs to the garden of his restaurant and (above) harvesting greens from his vegetable garden.

*Dinner at the granite
table outside at
Franco's.*

around. The house in fact belongs to Franco's mother-in-law, who lives in one wing, while her three daughters and their families live in their own areas in other wings of the house.

Behind, on a small hillside and bathed in sunlight, is the vegetable garden. It is surprisingly small for something that has not only to feed three families, but supply the restaurant. All the greens are in organised rows. There is a wide variety of plants and many rows of the same plant, all in different stages of maturity. In this way, Franco can keep a supply of salads and other essentials going all through summer.

Franco and I – he with a large basket – move through the garden as he rapidly cuts a green harvest for the night's dinner. His knowledge of the plants, their fertiliser needs, their health, their likes and dislikes is impressive. It is a real practitioner's skill – the chef who understands how to grow his own food.

The harvest collected, we sit under a small pergola in the shade of an old grapevine as Franco serves coffee and his own fresh lemonade. We savour the moment and keenly anticipate the pleasures of the evening ahead.

Later, just as the sun has set and the light is soft, we drive up to the restaurant and choose a table in the garden at the front under the branches of an ancient deodar. The table is made of one single slab of granite, typical of the Ticino everywhere. The Ticinese are great stonemasons and there is no shortage of granite to choose from in the gorges leading to the main peaks. From the garden there is a flight of stairs up to the main floor of the restaurant itself and, a moment later, Franco appears, resplendent in his chef's hat, at the top of the stairs. It's a rather grand entrance on to the beautiful stage of this setting, but Franco is an old hand on the stage and clearly enjoys the performance.

There follows a lively discussion about what we are to eat, in particular how we are going to enjoy the harvest of greens picked that afternoon from his garden. For the greens, in the end we decide that simplest is best and we choose a giant mixed leaf salad. This will be accompanied by the summer freshness of a fennel salad.

For our first course, Franco is making a gnocchi dish for which he is renowned and which he claims to have created. It is made from light potato dumplings which have inside them a small piece of fontina cheese. When cooked, the outsides of the gnocchi are firm, the insides runny and very cheesy. It is served with a classic tomato sauce.

To follow, we choose another of his specialities and a great favourite of mine: Vitello Tonnato, cold veal with a tuna–mayonnaise sauce. Franco also does a simple dish substituting onions for the veal. We indulge and have both veal and onions with a large bowl of the sauce. The mixed salad and fennel will follow.

At this point there is a lively debate about the choice of wine. We are looking for a local merlot and my father is keen on a wine called San Zeno, a wine so local that you would probably see the vineyard if you stood on Franco's roof. But Franco is sold out of San Zeno and he recommends a merlot from Villa Jelmini. Augusto takes a little convincing as it is almost a foreign wine, coming as it does from a valley near Locarno, some 40 km away. In the end he is convinced and, on tasting, we all agree the wine seems to have survived the journey from Locarno without mishap.

The combination of the local wine, the home-grown food, Franco's culinary skills and the balmy summer evening in the garden is simple and perfect.

Gnocchi
DI PATATE CON *Fonduta*
POTATO GNOCCHI WITH CHEESE

1 kg (2 lb 3 oz) floury potatoes,
e.g. King Edward

300 g (10½ oz) plain
(all-purpose) flour

salt

150 g (5 oz) fontina cheese

Boil potatoes in their jackets until tender.
While still hot, peel them and push them through
a 'ricer', or mash them with a fork. Now add the flour
and salt and make into a dough. The less flour you
can incorporate, the better, otherwise the gnocchi
become hard. The dough must be soft but not stick
to your hands.

Break off a piece of dough and roll into a snake about
1.5 cm (½ in) in diameter. Cut the fontina cheese into
matchstick-size sticks. With a knife, make a groove
in the potato snake, push the cheese into the groove
and roll. Now cut the snake into 1.5 cm (½ in) long
pieces. Put on a floured tray.

Put a large pot of salted water to boil. Drop the
gnocchi in a few at a time. When they come to the
surface, they are cooked. Lift them out with a sieve
or slotted spoon and put on a warmed serving plate.
Pour tomato sauce (see next recipe) over them and
serve with fresh parmigiano on the side.

Serves 4–6

Salsa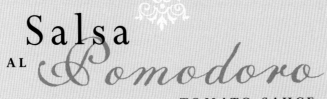

AL Pomodoro

TOMATO SAUCE

1 Spanish onion, chopped

2–3 cloves garlic, chopped

sage leaves

1 bay leaf

150 g (5 oz) tomato paste

500 g (1 lb 2 oz) ripe, peeled Roma tomatoes (canned tomatoes can be used if fresh are not available)

salt and pepper

1 small chilli (optional)

basil leaves

This is the basic recipe for tomato sauce.

In a bit of butter and virgin olive oil, let onion soften and become transparent. Add garlic, sage and bay leaves (or you can use thyme, oregano or rosemary if you prefer).

Add the tomato paste and mix it all well, cooking until the paste turns a terracotta colour (do not let it burn). Then add the tomatoes, mix well, add salt and pepper as required or a small chilli pepper. Cover and cook for about 20 minutes, stirring often. Finally, chop basil leaves and add to the dish.

Note

The tomato paste gives the sauce a richer, stronger flavour.

Serves 4–6 people

Vitello Tonnato

VEAL WITH TUNA–MAYONNAISE

1 veal nut (noix or topside), wrapped very tight in a cheesecloth

250 ml (8½ fl oz) dry white wine

1–2 large carrots, cut into large pieces

1–2 celery sticks, cut into large pieces

1 large onion, cut into large pieces

2 bay leaves

a few peppercorns

MAYONNAISE

2 egg yolks

1 teaspoon salt

300 ml (10 fl oz) sunflower oil

juice of ½ lemon

1 teaspoon Dijon mustard

TUNA MIX

500 g (1 lb 2 oz) canned tuna

10 anchovies

handful of capers

salt and pepper

Choose a saucepan that the veal will just fit into. Put veal in pan and cover with cold water. Add the wine, carrots, celery, onion, bay leaves and peppercorns. Put the lid on. Bring to the boil and then reduce heat to low; let it simmer for about 30 minutes. Allow the meat to cool in the broth and retain broth.

Meanwhile, prepare a mayonnaise. Beat the egg yolks with salt and mustard, then while continuing to beat steadily add the oil drop by drop; as the yolks begin to thicken increase the oil to a steady trickle. Add lemon juice and taste for seasoning.

Put tuna, anchovies and capers in a food processor, pulse to mix and add 1–2 ladlefuls of the veal broth. The tuna mix should be like a thick cream. Taste and add pepper and salt if needed.

Slice the veal very thinly and arrange on a serving plate. Mix some mayonnaise with the tuna mixture, spread some of it over the sliced meat and put the rest in a bowl, to serve on the side. Decorate with capers.

Note

The stock that results from cooking the veal can be used to make risotto! It can be frozen for later use.

Serves 6

Cipolline *Tonnate*

ONIONS WITH TUNA–MAYONNAISE

olive oil for sprinkling

10 small peeled onions

Preheat oven to 180–200°C (350–400°F).

Sprinkle some olive oil on 10 small peeled onions and put them on an oven tray. Bake until they are cooked, shaking the tray from time to time – about 15 minutes.

When cool put them on a serving dish and pour the vitello tonnato sauce over them.

Dressing
FOR SALADS AND *Vegetables*

juice of 1 large lemon

1 tablespoon Dijon mustard

1 teaspoon salt

freshly ground black pepper

approx. 200 ml (7 fl oz) extra-virgin olive oil

Put all ingredients in a glass jar with lid and shake very well.

Pour over:

- green beans that have been cooked in salted water and drained (should still be a bit al dente)
- fennel that has been sliced very finely, adding 2 tablespoons of baby capers
- zucchini (courgettes) sliced very finely
- arugula (rocket) salad with very fine slivers of parmigiano
- mixed salad.

Insalata
DI *Finocchio*
FENNEL SALAD

1 firm bulb of fennel

juice of 1 lemon

½ cup virgin olive oil

salt and pepper

handful of capers

Choose a male variety of fennel bulb — they are thinner, flatter and longer than the more rounded female ones. Cut in half lengthways and slice as thinly as possible. Make a sauce with the remaining ingredients, mixing well, and pour over fennel.

Serves 4

A Day IN THE Valle

ONE HUNDRED YEARS AGO, THE REMOTE VALLEYS OF SOUTHERN SWITZERLAND supported a patchwork of small villages where people lived on the little they could grow and the few animals they could keep. It was one of the poorest areas of Europe. The winters were harsh and long and the steep granite walls of the mountain ranges blocked sunlight for much of the day most of the year. Many villagers left for larger cities, such as Belinzona, the canton capital of Ticino, or Lugano. But mostly, they left to settle all over the world.

Today, these small villages are coming back to life – particularly in summer, when the chestnut woods are thick with new leaves and in the small fields a carpet of summer flowers grows through long lush grass, as every plant, bush and tree vies to make the most of the short span of warmth and sun. This is the period of bounty which makes survival possible. Hay can be cut and stored, animals are taken from their barns to the 'alti pascoli', the high mountain pastures. The rich milk from the summer grasses is made into the famous valley cheeses, meat is turned into salamis and prosciutto or the local 'carne secca', an air-dried beef. Hardy grapes are made into the local wine. In a good year it is a season of plenty, a brief pause to enjoy and relax in a life that was traditionally hard and often on the edge of tipping into real adversity.

Left: An old church above Lake Lugano. Above: An old stable with walls and roof tiles of granite.

This is the background for the great local tradition of the 'grotto' – a very simple rustic eating place set in one of these remote valleys. The grotto started out as a storehouse of summer produce – an early form of refrigeration. The cheeses, wines and cured meats needed to be kept cool in the summer months so many families made small chambers in the cool granite of the hillsides, often by icy streams, to store all this goodness. These storehouses evolved over time and developed an attached room for cold weather and tables under spreading trees for the warmer days. Today, in the age of home refrigeration, they have evolved further, into small rustic eating places which are visited by those who live in the cities as well as the locals, for a lunch or a long summer evening. The social customs are preserved, even if the original purpose has changed. A day visiting a grotto is one of the great traditions in this part of Switzerland.

So, on a perfect summer day, we – Augusto, Luca and his wife Gabi, my husband Michele and I – set off by car to an old favourite in the Valle di Blenio. It's a 40-minute drive up the main autostrada, past the turn-off to Locarno, past Belinzona with its three sentinel castles, and up to the junction of the valley that leads to the

San Gottardo Pass, the main road to the north. Instead of going to San Gottardo we turn left up the Valle di Blenio and soon we are off the main road and winding along the side of the valley, through small villages with their stone houses, granite roofs, and terraced fields all softened by an explosion of leaves and flowers and bathed in bright sunlight. Far above are the peaks of the Alps, bare now of their winter snow, and below them the sub-alpine world of the alti pascoli, the high pastures.

There are walking tracks all through these mountains and, being Switzerland, they are very well organised. Small yellow signs mark these tracks and tell you how far it is – in minutes or hours of walking – to the next village. Along the floor of the valley are rushing streams flowing over rounded granite boulders. The water looks tempting enough to go down for a quick swim, as it is as clear and fresh as the first day on earth. But don't be deceived – the water is breath-snatchingly icy, coming by sunless passages from the snow melt far above.

Our first stop is the Grotto Milani at Ludiano. There we have booked the top table – literally, for it is set in the branches of a spreading chestnut tree. The road climbs and twists through the village until after one final tight turn you arrive at a

Far left: The 'top table'
in the chestnut tree at
Grotto Milani.
Middle: Typical grotto
granite tables.

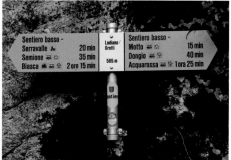

From top to bottom:
Mountain house with a
maize granary on the
top floor; Walking track
sign, showing times
instead of distances to
various destinations;
Mountain grape arbour;
Old timber slab walls of
a typical mountain house.
Far right: Typical house
of the valle, made of
stone and timber.

small flat area with the grotto on one side. Behind it are the crumpled stone remains of the old family storehouses, now no longer in use. Climbing a small flight of wooden steps, like a ladder propped against the tree, we arrive at a wooden platform with a long table surrounded by benches and rails. You look out through the leaves to the houses and valley below and across, not far away, are the steep slopes of the other side of the valley.

Far below in the valley is a large *belle epoque* villa with a tower, much grander than the rest, set in a park of century-old monkey puzzle and magnolia trees. It is probably the mansion of a returned emigrant who, having made his fortune in the New World, returned to show it off in his village. Like many of the houses in these valleys, it has survived by neglect in the period between when the population shrank dramatically through emigration and today, when the houses have been restored and cared for by a new generation, who value this wild scenery in the heart of Europe.

The menu in a grotto is traditional, simple and short. We have a minestrone soup to start, followed by a plate of cured meats – salamis, ham, carne secca – and a selection of mountain cheeses. This is washed down with small china jugs, called 'boccalini', of the local red wine.

The wine is Cios di Conigudo and is made, preservative-free, by a local farmer. It is traditionally mixed with 'gazosa', a sweet lemonade. This sounds an odd mix but in that setting, with that food, it works. Gazosa probably improves some of the local wines, as they are as rough and austere as some of the scenery.

After lunch we drive a short distance to the other side of the same village and our next grotto – the Grotto Spruch. 'Spruch' in the local dialect is a shelter where you keep goats safe for the winter. It is remarkable because the whole of the inside of the grotto – kitchen, bar and tables – is fitted under the overhang of a giant rock shelf. In winter this would be cosy and must arouse all sorts of long-buried tribal memories of warmth, safety and caves. On a summer day you need to be outside so we take caffè under a grape arbour nearby. The pergola is slightly austere – granite-paved with stone benches, stone table and stone supports for the pergola itself – but has a wide view of the fields and valley below.

Later, we drive down the valley, cross the river and finally get to the village of Biasca. Just outside Biasca is the site of a famous line of grottos dug into the hillside above a fast-flowing stream. Originally there were over 150 grotti, one for each family in the village. Now about 10 small grotto restaurants remain, every one with a large terrace set under the spreading branches of old plane trees. Under each tree is a group of stone tables, each one of which, originally, also belonged to a

From left to right: Gazosa bottle; Wine in the ciottola; Lunch plate of cheese and cured meats with ciottola and boccalino for the wine; Field flowers; Caffè at Grotto Spruch.

particular family. Behind each grotto, in and usually down a flight of steps, remain the storerooms which were their original purpose. These are still hung with salamis and cheeses, there are flagons of local wine and now, in a meeting of the old and new in refrigeration, there are usually freezers for home-made ice creams. We sample the ice creams and, as usual, I find I prefer the local 'nocciola' (hazelnut), which has a rich nutty taste and should not be too sweet. After strolling around the valley we head back to Lugano and our final encounter with the world of the grotto – dinner at the Grotto Posmonte.

On the ridges above Lake Lugano there are small villages, now edged with smart villas that date from 150 years ago to the present time. The views are spectacular, down to the lake itself or across valleys to the Alps. The road winds up to these ridges and then follows their narrow forms until finally, some 400 metres above the lake, we arrive at the Grotto Posmonte near the village of Agra. It is set in a beech forest with old trees so dense that nothing grows beneath them. It is a shaded secret world of leaf-mould and dappled light – very much the enchanted forest of European fairy tales.

The grotto is a little larger than normal and has a generous wooden deck set some 3 metres above ground level. To one side is a long 'boccia' pit with benches beside it for the traditional afternoon game of bowls. On the other side you look out through the beech trees to glimpses of the distant views beyond.

We go here because the food is really excellent: simplicity itself but with a refinement of execution that a grand restaurant would be proud of. On the menu today are wild mushrooms with polenta, a marvellous polenta with melted cheese, pappardelle pasta with a ragù and the classic of cucina povera, Pasta e Fagioli – pasta and beans.

Of course, at the end of such a dinner, you have to have a 'digestivo', or digestive liqueur. The two favourites here are either the local grappa (which is delicious, mellow and scented like mown hay) or the famous ratafià, as the locals call it, or 'nocino', as it is known elsewhere. Ratafià, allegedly invented – as were many other famous liqueurs and wines – by monks, is an inky-black drink made from green walnuts. The name apparently derives from the Latin phrase *rata fiat*, meaning, loosely, 'it's approved, let it be done', with which the monks used to wind

Village scenes from the Valle Si Blenio

up a formal business discussion. Purely for the good of our stomachs we try both and find them excellent. But the ratafià is more unusual, more typical of the place, so that is the bottle that gets left on the table and well sampled.

As we come down the mountain and head for home, we drive into lightning and thunder which turns into torrential rain by the time we reach the house. It is wild and spectacular, as the thunderclaps echo around the mountain walls and peaks and valleys appear out of the darkness in strobe-light flashes. The monsters who live in the jagged peaks above the forest are restless. Although we have had an enchanted day in the valleys and basked in the soft lushness of summer, the storm is a reminder that in the mountains nothing can be taken for granted. You live on the edge of a wild world and this gives a special glow to the day in the valle which we have just enjoyed.

Polenta con Formaggio Fuso – polenta with melted cheese – is a delicious and simple way to prepare polenta. Slices of fairly strong-tasting cheeses, such as fontina and gorgonzola, are sandwiched between two layers of very hot polenta and then eaten immediately. The mix of the hot, grainy polenta with the cooler, partly melted cheese is an inspired combination.

My mother used to make a rich and tantalising ragù to go with her pappardelle, so there also is my recipe for the pasta and her sauce and it is called after her – Pappardelle 'Sciura Toti'.

The third recipe is for the classic Pasta e Fagioli.

Polenta *Fuso*
CON FORMAGGIO
POLENTA WITH MELTED CHEESE

**1 quantity polenta
(see basic recipe page 15)**

**6–8 slices of cheese, such as
gorgonzola or fontina**

*This is a very simple dish and is often eaten for
lunch in the grotti. You can use any of your favourite
cheeses for this dish, but they should melt easily.
I like using gorgonzola, fontina or the mountain
cheeses produced in the Ticino.*

Make the polenta following the basic recipe.

Put a nice big slice of very hot polenta on your
plate. Cut a piece of cheese and put on top of the
polenta. It will start to melt very quickly and the
dish is ready.

Serves 6–8

Pappardelle 'SCIURA Toti'

6 eggs

720 g (1 lb 9 oz) plain
(all-purpose) flour (see Note)

2 teaspoons salt

RAGÙ

600 g (1 lb 5 oz) meat
of your choice

15–20 g (½–¾oz) dried porcini
mushrooms, sliced

1 large red onion, chopped

2–3 cloves garlic, chopped

approx. 10 sage leaves

rosemary

2 fresh bay leaves

250 ml (8½ fl oz) dry red wine

2–3 generous tablespoons
tomato paste

600 g (1 lb 5 oz) tomatoes,
peeled (fresh or canned)

*For this dish it is really worthwhile to make your own pappardelle – this is
flat, broad ribbon pasta. The more flour you can incorporate into the eggs,
the better the pasta will be: aim for 100–120 g (3–4 oz) flour per egg.
Traditionally, this dish was made with wild boar, but you can use any meat
you wish – veal, beef, duck, rabbit, hare, chicken or pork …*

Put eggs, flour and salt into a food processor and mix using a dough hook
until the pasta is elastic (about 5 minutes).

Feed pasta through pasta machine, on widest setting, then fold flattened wide
ribbon of pasta into three and repeat process 3–5 times. Reduce setting and
repeat process until you get to third last setting. Cut the ribbons into 3 cm
(1½ in) wide pappardelle and hang them over a floured broom handle.

Cut meat into fine small pieces. I prefer not to mince the meat so you can
find little pieces in the sauce. Soak the porcini mushrooms until they have
plumped up.

In a saucepan with a bit of butter and olive oil, let onion and garlic cook
until golden, add herbs and the meat and let meat brown for a few minutes,
then add 1 glass dry red wine and stir until it has evaporated.

Add tomato concentrate to the meat mixture and cook for another
3–4 minutes, then add peeled tomatoes, the porcini mushrooms and
some of the water used for soaking them. Mix all well, turn the heat
very low and stir from time to time. Cover and cook for about 1 hour.

Bring a big saucepan with salted water to the boil. Drop in the pappardelle
and cook for about 2 minutes. Drain and mix with the ragù.

Note

*Unbleached flour should be used, but best of all is Italian flour designed for pasta:
farina Tipo '00'. Try speciality shops or Italian grocers and delicatessens.*

Serves 6

Pasta E *Fagioli*

PASTA AND BEANS

250 g (9 oz) dried borlotti beans, soaked overnight, or 400 g (14 oz) fresh beans

150 g (5 oz) pancetta, diced

2 large red onions, sliced

2–3 sticks celery, sliced

2–3 carrots, sliced

2–3 cloves garlic, chopped

1 chilli

sage, bay leaves, rosemary, Italian parsley

4–6 pork sausages (optional), chopped into 2 cm (¾ in) lengths

1 glass dry red or white wine

500 ml (generous pint) fresh chicken or veal stock

800 g (1 lb 12 oz) peeled plum tomatoes

500 g (1 lb 2 oz) short pasta, e.g. shells

salt and freshly ground black pepper

If you are using fresh beans, they do not require any soaking.

In a large saucepan fry the pancetta, sliced onion, celery, carrot, garlic and whole chilli. Add herbs.

If using, add the sausages and cook for a few minutes until the sausages start to brown. Now add the wine, stirring vigorously until it evaporates. Add the chicken or veal stock, then the drained borlotti beans and tomatoes. Let it all cook for about 30–45 minutes, covered, or until the borlotti are very tender.

Now add the pasta. If the dish looks dry at this point add more stock or water (the finished dish should be quite moist, and the pasta will take up liquid). Cook until the pasta is al dente or about 10–12 minutes, depending on what pasta you use. Taste for salt and pepper and season.

Serve with freshly grated parmigiano and a little virgin olive oil on the table.

Serves 6–8

Giretto
DEL *Lago*

CITIES BUILT ON LAKES OR BY THE SEA HAVE A PARTICULAR CHARACTERISTIC — they all are focused on the water like a sunflower following the sun and, in a subtle way, turn their back on the land. To be the object of their gaze you have to go out on the water.

I have always loved the lake. In my childhood the waters were clean and sparkling and we used to go swimming from the small, gravelly beach near the city known as the Lido. It was where my mother swam often in her teenage years. In those days, there were few boats on the lake and many of them were the old wooden two-ended craft like gondolas which had a canvas over the top supported by hoops. These were used by fishermen and also for transport in the times when water was the quickest way from one place to another.

Nowadays, large lake ferries ply the waters with a host of other pleasure craft and the gondolas are no more. There is a nostalgic wooden launch you can hire for a tour, all varnish and polished brass, and it is this boat we take for our day on the lake.

Lake Lugano is a lesser known member of that group of sub-alpine lakes across the north of Italy that includes the more famous Como, Maggiore and Garda. For the most part, the northern sides of the lake are steep and drop sharply from high

Left: A storehouse with its boatshed at Cantina di Gandria.
Above: Gandria.

up into the waters. They are covered in chestnut woods which give the whole area a particularly wild character. It is not over-built because it is too steep, so its natural beauty has been preserved.

At various points along the lake, large villas have been constructed surrounded by splendid and rather exotic gardens that fitted the imagination of their owners, who saw the lake as some sort of exotic semi-tropical paradise. Most of these villas were built in the second half of the nineteenth century, after the completion of the railway tunnel from the north; the influx of northerners that resulted began the transformation of Lugano's fortunes from a sleepy lakeside town to the present-day city.

The star of these villas, the biggest, grandest and most elegant, set in the largest garden on the best site, is an earlier building. It is called the Villa Favorita and has been, until recently, the home of Baron Heinrich von Thyssen-Bornemisza and his legendary art collection. Villa Favorita dates from the early eighteenth century – a time when Lugano would have been a village and there were no other grand houses on the lake – so it is a palace in a private paradise. Many of the villas on Lago di Como date from the same period and would have had the same feel. Those were the days before tourism, when only the very rich could afford to move their

establishments for part of the year. Communication would have been by boat and you can see docks and boatsheds along Villa Favorita's long lakeside wall.

Villa Favorita also has the most magical garden, in the late nineteenth-century English landscape style with deodars, monkey puzzles, magnolia grandifloras and palms. It has a long drive bordered by Italian cypress – pencil pines – underplanted with iris, with a low wall festooned with old wisteria on one side. It has to be one of the great garden settings of the world. Nowadays the only way to see it, beautiful but not quite the same experience, is from the water, as we do on our boat trip.

Chugging further along the lake we come to Gandria, one of two picturesque villages on its shores. Gandria is all small-scale, rather plain houses clinging, one on top of the other, to an impossibly steep wall of rock. At the water's edge are the boats and wharves of the houses which go straight down to the lake. Here and there small gardens appear on narrow terraces planted not with the grand villa trees, but with olives, vines, fruit trees, citrus and loquats – things you can use and eat.

Opposite Gandria, on the northern side of the lake and in almost permanent shadow from the mountains above, is a chain of buildings known as Cantine di Gandria, or Gandria's cellars. They are really grotti, the spot chosen because it was

*Above: Views from
the boat.
Right: The lake shore at
Cantina di Gandria.*

always in shade and cool, so here the wine and other produce was stored. Like the mountain grotti, they have evolved with outdoor tables under spreading trees for warm days and nights when you want to eat outside in a tranquil setting. In my grandfather's day he would row across here for lunch. Now we glide swiftly by on our way to the other village, right at the other end of the lake, called Morcote, where we plan to arrive for lunch.

Steaming up the lake on our way to Morcote we turn our eyes away from the ugliness of Campione – a land-locked piece of Italy in Switzerland. Campione is dominated by its casino and a new, even larger one, is now being built by Lugano's renowned and favourite son architect, Mario Botta. Botta's casino, no doubt as per his brief, is hugely out of scale with the town that surrounds it, a real temple of Mammon, so it's best to hurry on by.

Morcote is beautifully sited at the foot of the southern slopes of Mt San Salvatore, on a promontory at the end of the lake. The village starts at the water's edge and straggles its way along narrow paths up the hill which is dominated at its crest by an old church with a high tower. The terraces between the church and the village are a genuine micro-climate, taking the full force of the sun, which heats the rocks behind them to provide ambient warmth on cold nights. They are covered with lush and exotic gardens, one or two quite renowned.

At the end of the lake, the houses of Morcote are built over a long, generous colonnade which today has a host of small shops, stalls and restaurants. Between the lake and the colonnade is a narrow road (the only place you could build it) and on the other side of the road are floating platforms topped with pergolas of canvas or wisteria, and set with tables. Here you can eat in a true al fresco setting, as your waiter dodges the passing cars to bring you your order from the restaurants on the land. We pull up alongside one of these platforms and go 'ashore' for lunch.

We decide to order something light, accompanied by various salads or vegetables. We can't decide between two delicious dishes here – one of eggs, cream and ham baked in a ramekin, known as Uova in Cocotte, and a light gnocchi made from semolina, Gnocchi alla Romana. So we try both and have with them some of my favourite salads: Carpaccio di Zucchini (raw zucchini with oil and lemon), mushroom salad, a salad of cauliflower and anchovies and a green bean salad. They are exceptional and the essence of al fresco eating. As we are a large group, we order all these plates and everyone tries everything. The sharing is as much part of the experience as is the food.

Heading back up the lake to Lugano and home, we motor into a stiff, cold breeze that has come down the valley from the mountains above. It is a reminder that these moments of warmth and companionship are precious.

Uova
IN *Cocotte*
EGGS IN COCOTTE

12 slices pancetta

1½ large Spanish onions

600 g (1 lb 5 oz) frozen chopped
spinach, drained

salt and freshly ground
black pepper

12 organic large eggs

250 ml (8½ fl oz) cream

150 g (5 oz) grated parmigiano

unsalted butter

You need one large ovenproof ramekin or bowl per person.
Preheat oven to 200°C (400°F). Fry pancetta in a pan
until crisp in a small amount of oil then let it drain on
a paper towel.

Chop onions and let them soften in a bit of butter
and oil. Add the well-drained spinach, salt and pepper
and cook for a few minutes. Add the pancetta.

Butter the ramekins, spread the spinach mixture
evenly between the 6 bowls. Make a small indentation
and break 2 whole eggs into each dish, being careful
not to break the egg yolks. Add about 2 tablespoons
of cream on top of the eggs in each bowl, season with
salt and pepper and scatter parmigiano over the top.
Lastly, add a small knob of unsalted butter to each.
Bake in oven for about 5–8 minutes. The egg yolks
should still be soft when they are served.

Serves 6

Gnocchi

ALLA *Romana*

ROMAN GNOCCHI

1 litre (2 pints) milk

½ litre (1 pint) water

salt

250 g (9 oz) coarse semolina

2 egg yolks

freshly ground black pepper

1 cup grated parmigiano

2–3 tablespoons fresh breadcrumbs

approx. 100 g (3½ oz) butter

fresh sage leaves

Put milk and water on stove in a large pan, add 1–2 teaspoons of salt and bring to the boil. Add semolina slowly, in a very fine and constant stream, whisking continuously so as not to form lumps. Let cook for about 10 minutes, stirring constantly with a wooden spoon. Then let the semolina cool slightly.

Taste for salt, stir in the egg yolks, pepper and about half the parmigiano.

Put some greaseproof paper on your kitchen bench or table and pour the semolina on to the paper, flattening it with the blade of a knife to about 1 cm (½ in) thickness. Let it cool completely.

Preheat oven to 200°C (400°F) and butter an ovenproof dish, about 5–6 cm (2–2½ in) deep. With a biscuit cutter or a glass of about 3 cm (1¼ in) diameter, cut out little discs of the semolina mixture; arrange them in the dish, letting the discs overlap slightly, like fish scales.

Sprinkle breadcrumbs and the rest of the parmigiano on top of the semolina discs. Cut butter into little cubes and place on top of gnocchi and, finally, the sage leaves. Bake in oven for about 20 minutes, or until golden brown.

Variations

To this basic recipe, you can add about 400 g (14 oz) finely chopped spinach to the milk. The gnocchi then becomes green.

Alternatively, add about 300 g (10 oz) baked, mashed pumpkin.

These gnocchi will be softer than the basic recipe, therefore a little more difficult to handle, but the sweetness of the pumpkin is absolutely delicious.

Serves 4

Carpaccio *di Zucchini*

ZUCCHINI SALAD

3–4 small zucchini
(courgettes), thinly sliced

juice of 1 lemon

½ cup virgin olive oil

salt and freshly ground black
pepper to taste

1 small fresh chilli, deseeded
and finely chopped

*Choose very young, small zucchini (courgettes)
and slice very thinly.*

Mix the lemon juice, virgin olive oil, salt and pepper
and a small fresh chilli, with seeds removed. Pour
dressing over zucchini, and let rest for about
15 minutes before serving.

Serves 4

Insalata
DI *Funghi*
MUSHROOM SALAD

300 g (10½ oz) whole small button mushrooms

juice of half a lemon

½ cup virgin olive oil

salt and freshly ground black pepper to taste

1 fresh chilli, finely chopped

½ bunch of flat-leaved Italian parsley, chopped

Take small button mushrooms (the smaller the better) and clean any dirt from around their stems with a paper towel.

In a bowl mix lemon juice, virgin olive oil, salt and pepper, chilli and Italian parsley. Mix in the mushrooms. Leave to marinate for at least 20 minutes before serving.

Serves 4

Insalata
DI *Faggiolini*
GREEN BEAN SALAD

500 g (1 lb 2 oz) small, green beans

1-2 cloves of garlic, crushed

⅓ cup of red wine vinegar

½ cup of virgin olive oil

salt and freshly ground black pepper to taste

Top and tail the very small green beans. Put the salted water in a saucepan, bring to the boil and add the beans, cooking until still crunchy. Drain quickly and rinse under cold water to prevent them cooking further.

In a bowl put the crushed garlic, red wine vinegar, virgin olive oil, salt and pepper. Mix well and add the beans. If you like, you can add some chopped arugula (rocket) leaves to the bean salad.

Serves 4

Insalata
DI Cavolfiore
CAULIFLOWER SALAD

1 small cauliflower

½ cup of red wine vinegar

1 cup virgin olive oil

4–5 anchovy fillets, mashed

1 fresh chilli, finely chopped

1 handful of flat-leaved Italian parsley, chopped

Choose a very firm, white cauliflower, removing all the green leaves. Divide the cauliflower into florets. Put some salted water in a saucepan and bring to the boil. Drop the florets into the water and boil for only a few minutes. They should still be very firm. Rinse them under the cold water to prevent them cooking further then dry on paper towel.

In a bowl mix the red wine vinegar with the virgin olive oil then add anchovies and chillies. Pour over cauliflower and top with chopped Italian parsley.

Serves 4

The magic
OF THE COSTA *Smeralda*

FROM LUGANO AND SOUTHERN SWITZERLAND, WE ARE ABOUT TO TRAVEL TO the next stage of my trip … to the remote north-east coast of the island of Sardegna. The small plane leaves Lugano airport and almost instantly is out over the flat plains of Lombardy and the silver snake of the River Po. This has been rich agricultural country from earliest times. Even today it is productive land, famous for growing arborio rice (the basis of the north Italian risottos) and corn for polenta.

Then we pass over the Mediterranean coast near the great port city of Genova and fly out over an impossibly dark blue sea flecked with white from the prevailing winds. Far out to the left we see a distant glimpse of the island of Elba, Napoleon's first place of exile, then on the right-hand side of the aircraft the rugged eastern coast of Corsica with its high central mountains. Soon we are swooping down over the buff Sardegnan landscape, out over the water then landing at the airport of the northern port city of Olbia – gateway to the fabled Costa Smeralda, or emerald coast.

Today's Costa Smeralda is the work of a group of wealthy yachtsmen who in the 1950s used to visit the rugged coast of Gallura in the north east of Sardegna. In those days there was nothing on the coast itself – no towns, no services, no ports, no villages. Life, hard and often dangerous, was lived inland in the valleys, with

Left: Stella Maris church, Porto Cervo on the Costa Smerelda. Above: Traditional Sardegnan fishing boats.

Off to shop in the old family car.

subsistence farming and a strong seasoning of banditry. Cows would occasionally graze where today the gardens of famous villas run down to the water. On a trip to this remote coast, one of the poorest regions in Western Europe, these travellers decided to form a group to develop the coast as a holiday resort. It was to be a development with a difference, with far-sighted policies on environmental controls, strict building codes and no over-building. The concept was married to World Bank funding and the Costa Smeralda Consortium was born.

From its first days, its chairman and guiding light was Prince Karim Aga Khan, world leader of the Ismaili Muslims, the scion of a large fortune and the grandson of the man whose name is in the Libro d'Oro of the Ristorante Biaggi. Some 40 years on, the Costa Smeralda has grown enormously, but is sticking to its early ideas of controlled development and the Aga Khan still comes each year for the summer, presiding over the famous Yacht Club Costa Smeralda at Porto Cervo, just across the water from his villa. The figure of the Aga Khan, the 'Principe' as he is known locally, is indelibly associated with the Costa Smeralda and did much, particularly in its early years, to encourage the rich and famous of European society to establish grand villas in this unknown and remote area.

*Mediterranean
vernacular architecture
is the style of the
Costa Smeralda.*

The Costa Smeralda Consortium bought some 20 kilometres of rugged coastline and the hinterland behind it for a kilometre or two. Its centre is the port of Porto Cervo, built from scratch, as were the early and beautiful hotels of Pitrizza, Cala di Volpe, Porto Cervo and Romazzino. Gradually, the villas, the services, the restaurants, bars and shops followed. What had once been poor sheep country has become one of the famous coastal playgrounds of Europe.

A story is told that along the way this development created some rich Sardegnan women. The land the consortium bought on the coast was long considered the poorest land for agricultural purposes – the better country was inland. The poorer land, as often as not, was given to the girls in the family. When it came to be developed and appreciated for something other than its original purpose, the tables were turned and these girls became rich. Their brothers had to wait longer to prosper as the region developed.

My mother and father had been searching for some time for a place to build a family holiday house by the sea. They had looked all over the Western Mediterranean and had even spent some summers camping on the Sardegnan coast.

About 30 years ago, they fell in love with the remote rugged coast of the Costa Smeralda and decided they would buy some land and build there. Thus our house, called 'Lu Nibaru' – the Sardegnan word for the low prostrate juniper that grows in the area – was born.

It is a simple, low white-washed house of four bedrooms built very much in the Mediterranean, vernacular style with white walls, terracotta tiles and exposed wooden beams. It has two matchless virtues – it is about 50 metres from a small sandy beach and it has a beautiful roof terrace covering over half the area of the house. From the roof you look out over the bay of Liscia di Vacca, across to the island of Caprera and, beyond that again, on a clear day, the high peaks of Corsica. Behind, looking inland, are high granite escarpments and peaks – a wild and rugged landscape of primitive beauty.

I have been coming here for over 30 years, even before Lu Nibaru was built. Since then I have managed to visit most years. For my three children, it forms part of their childhood and they holiday here still, whenever they can, from wherever in the world they are living.

Top: View over Liscia di Vacca towards the island of Maddalena. Above: Hotel Cala di Volpe.

They say smell is the strongest trigger for memory and the wild coast of Sardegna has its own unforgettable scent. As you drive north from Olbia towards the Costa Smeralda, windows down so the warm air washes over the people in the car, there comes a point after you have left the outskirts of town and as you get the first glimpses of the sea, when your senses are almost assaulted by a wave of scents. This is the perfume of the 'macchia', the low coastal scrub of cistus, juniper and strawberry trees, all plants that release their essential oils in the heat. All your memories of summer come flooding back – the holiday has begun.

After three decades we have our favourite places, our everyday rituals, our favourite foods and a group of locals whom we enjoy seeing year after year. Over the next week or so we plan to do all those things and go to all those places, and enjoy al fresco living on the Costa Smeralda.

On our first night we all want to eat something typically Sardegnan and so choose three old favourites. For the first course we have Bottarga con Sedano – bottarga with celery. Bottarga is the smoked fish roe found in many parts of the Mediterranean and is famous in Sardegna. It can be made from tuna or grey mullet (*muggine*) and I firmly prefer the latter, which has a bright terracotta colour. The strong flavour and colour of the bottarga, sliced in thin strips on the pale crispy freshness of the celery, is a sensational marriage of contrasts.

We then choose another Sardegnan dish – Culligiones. Culligiones are the Sardegnan version of ravioli, large pasta cushions filled with potato and wild mint, an unusual and very satisfying mixture. They should be served as simply as possible with melted butter, parmigiano cheese and a little sage.

To refresh the palate at the end and to start the summer off, we have a favourite local ice cream – Semifreddo di Miele Amaro, a soft ice cream flavoured with the unique Sardegnan bitter honey, made from 'corbezzolo' – the local variant of the Irish strawberry tree. The bitter-sweet mix of the honey and the semifreddo is most unusual and is an exotic combination.

Inland from the Costa Smeralda is the Gallura, a well-known wine-growing region. The wines are mostly light and summery, the whites and the rosés the most enjoyable. (More of this later when I visit the local winery, Tenuta di Capichera.) On our first night we enjoy a local rosato (rosé) called Oleandro (oleander), dry and fruity and a marvellous pale tint of oleander pink. It's great to be back!

Semifreddo

DI MIELE *Amaro*

BITTER HONEY SEMIFREDDO

6 egg yolks

150 g (5 oz) sugar

4–5 tablespoons honey of corbezzolo (see Note)

500 ml (1 pint) cream

3 egg whites

pinch of salt

100 g (3½oz) roasted almonds or pistachios

Soften honey by putting jar into a basin of hot water.
Beat sugar and egg yolks together until light and
fluffy. Add warmed honey.
Beat cream until stiff. Beat egg whites until stiff.
Roughly chop almonds or pistachios.
Mix everything together and freeze for about 6 hours.
Serve with some more bitter honey drizzled over
the semifreddo.

Note

*Corbezzolo is the wild strawberry tree that grows all over
Sardegna. It makes a bitter honey. If you can't find this
honey, you can use chestnut honey, but it will not have
the original's bitterness.*

Serves 8

Bottarga
CON *Pedano*
SMOKED FISH ROE WITH CELERY

1 smoked mullet fish roe	*At the fish market buy mullet fish roe.*
6–8 celery sticks	*It comes usually as two dried long sacs.*
juice of ½ lemon	Slice celery sticks very thinly and arrange on
virgin olive oil	individual dishes. On top of celery, slice the bottarga
freshly ground black pepper	very thinly, squeeze some lemon juice over it, then a
	drizzle of virgin olive oil and pepper.
	Serves 6

Culligiones
SARDINIAN
Ravioli

PASTA

440 g (15½ oz) plain (all-purpose) flour (see Note)

4 organic eggs

1 tablespoon olive oil

salt

extra flour for dusting pasta

FILLING

2 leeks, finely chopped

1 clove garlic, chopped

500 g (1 lb 2 oz) boiled and mashed potatoes

5–6 mint leaves (this is the original way, I prefer fresh sage leaves instead)

100 g (3½ oz) grated parmigiano

60 g (2 oz) Sardinian pecorino

salt and pepper

TOMATO SAUCE

1 quantity Salsa al Pomodoro, see page 61

Note

Unbleached flour should be used, but best of all is Italian flour designed for pasta: farina Tipo '00'. Try speciality shops or Italian grocers and delicatessens.

These are large ravioli — the recipe makes about 24.

Mix the flour, eggs, oil and salt in a food processor using a dough hook. When you get a nice, shiny ball of pasta, divide it into 4 or 5 portions and roll these out into strips with your pasta machine, starting at the thickest setting and rolling them five times, folding the sheets into three each time before you reroll. Then gradually reduce setting to the second finest number (my machine goes from 1 to 9, so the last rolling I do on 7).

For filling, gently fry leek and garlic together in a little butter and oil until they are soft and the leeks are sweet. Then mix all filling ingredients together. Make a tomato sauce.

Lay a pasta sheet on a surface dusted with flour. Put 1 tablespoon of filling on pasta, spaced out at about 5 cm (2 in). With a pastry brush dipped in water, very lightly wet around ravioli so that the pastry cover will stick better.

Cover with another pasta sheet, press down really well, then cut the ravioli in a round or square shape. They should be about 8–10 cm (3½–4 in) diameter. Make sure they are well sealed all round.

Lightly flour a tray and put the ravioli one next to the other on the tray. (At this stage they can be frozen, to be used on another day.)

Boil lots of salted water in a large saucepan. Drop the ravioli in. Cook for about 2–3 minutes. Test the pasta – it should be still a bit al dente.

Remove them one at a time and arrange 3–4 on individual dishes. Pour tomato sauce over culligiones and serve with some fresh parmigiano on the side.

Variation

Instead of tomato sauce, serve culligiones with burned sage butter and parmigiano. For burned sage butter, heat 100–150 g (3½–5 oz) unsalted butter over medium heat until it just turns light brown, then add 10–15 chopped sage leaves and allow to fry for 1–2 minutes.

Serves 6

In the Garden
AT
Lu Nibaru

AWAKING AFTER OUR FIRST NIGHT BACK IN SARDEGNA, I OPEN THE SHUTTERS and the morning light streams in. At times on this coast the winds can be a bit wild and woolly, but today all is still. If you are feeling energetic this is the moment to go down to the beach for an early morning swim. No one is there, the water laps quietly on the sand and, if there are one or two yachts at anchor out on the bay, there seems no sign of life on them.

I am not an early morning swimmer so my thoughts turn to coffee. I know the cupboard is empty, it's a beautiful day, so I plan to go out and buy the ingredients for lunch in the garden, to ease our way into the rhythm of life by the sea.

Up on the hill about a kilometre behind the house is the shopping centre of Liscia Ruja. There is a small supermarket and, importantly, a really excellent café, the Bar Spinnaker. At this time Bar Spinnaker is full of locals readying for the day. Most of the holidaymakers are still in bed. There is a newspaper shop next door, tables spilling out on to a terrace and a cappuccino maker who is a master of his art. There is an Italian saying about coffee, that the best coffee is *sedente* (drunk sitting down), *bollente* (boiling hot) *e costa niente* (is free). You can certainly sit down at Bar Spinnaker, but I like my cappuccino not too hot (it changes the taste of the milk)

Left: The red spiny artichokes which are best for a raw salad.

and, of course, you have to pay. It comes just right, with a low creamy hood of foam artfully finished with a heart-shaped mark on the brown coffee. A quick glance at the paper and I am ready to go to the supermarket, which has basic supplies and an excellent delicatessen.

Signora Anna, who runs the supermarket, is an old friend. In fact it was she, when she was working as a real estate agent, who sold my parents the land on which Lu Nibaru is built. I am looking for a selection of prosciutto and salamis and two special cheeses – a fresh sheep's ricotta which I am going to bake for lunch and one of the crowning glories of Italian cheese-making, the 'burrata'. The burrata is a large buffalo-milk mozzarella which is firm on the outside and has the consistency of a runny cream on the inside. It comes shaped in a largish white soft ball held together with some narrow bands of palm fronds which are tied at the top. The presentation is almost zen in its simplicity and rightness and the taste, with the combination of the firm and the soft cheese, is an indulgent delight.

I am in luck and fresh burrata is in that day, as well as the fresh ricotta. I buy a large piece of the famous Pecorino Sardo or Sardegnan sheep's milk cheese, some beautiful prosciutto which is almost sweet to taste and a great stock of the Sardegnan 'fogli di musica', or sheet music – a wafer-thin bread which will be lightly grilled, dribbled with olive oil and sprinkled with salt.

Finding really fresh fruit and vegetables in resort towns is always a bit of a challenge and the Costa Smeralda is no exception. From long experience I have found that the best produce is to be had from roadside vendors. I have in mind one in particular, a woman, Signora Fabiola Farris, who operates from a truck on the road just past the Porto Cervo turn-off. The truck is stationed where there is room for six or so cars to park and for most of the day a steady procession of people stop to sample her offerings, which are displayed in tiers on the open side of the truck or still in their wooden crates on the ground in front.

The quality of her produce is always excellent and the variety is really tempting. I find some beautiful tiny yellow plums with their leaves still attached that are as sweet as magic moments. There are fresh apricots and large blood plums. Every ingredient you could wish for in salads is there – the tomatoes seem almost luminously red and are warm from the vine. I am particularly pleased to find some salad artichokes. These are a little smaller than the regular variety, sometimes quite purple in colour, and have sharp spikes on the end of their leaves. Prepared raw in a salad with lemon and oil and covered with thin shavings of parmigiano cheese they are one of the great summer salads.

Gathering all my bounty together and after finishing yet another long discussion on the merits of a particular fruit or vegetable with the Signora Fabiola, I head home to prepare lunch.

At Lu Nibaru there are terraces at the front and rear of the house: which is used at any time depends on the prevailing wind. There is also the marvellous roof terrace but, during the heat of the day, the shade provided by the lower terraces is necessary. Today we decide to eat at the front of the house next to an old wind-pruned juniper under the shade of a market umbrella. The table and benches are local and are also made of juniper wood.

For lunch there are cheeses, the prosciutto and salads, together with the fogli di musica bread. This sounds simple but it is an indulgence. The burrata is perfect, the baked ricotta a tantalising balance between the ricotta and the parmigiano, and the artichoke salad is as good as Signora Fabiola promised. This is our first lunch for the summer and it is a tantalising introduction to the days and nights to come.

Far left: The lunch table at Lu Nibaru. Above, left to right: The burrata in its palm leaf wrapping; Sardegnan olives; A selection of Sardegnan sheep's milk cheeses.

Ricotta
AL *Forno*
BAKED RICOTTA

500 g (1 lb 2 oz) ricotta

2 eggs

100 g (3½ oz) parmigiano

a few fresh oregano leaves

salt and freshly
ground black pepper

Preheat oven to 200°C (400°F). Mix everything well together in a bowl. Butter an ovenproof dish, put mixture in this dish and bake for about 25 minutes. When it is golden and has puffed up, it is ready. You can eat it hot, but it has more flavour cold.

Serves 4

Fogli
DI *Musica*
SHEET MUSIC BREAD

pitta bread

olive oil

rosemary

Maldon sea salt

To make fogli di musica is a very long and complicated process. As a substitute you can buy pitta bread, split it in half, brush some olive oil on it, add rosemary and Maldon salt, then put it under the grill (broiler) for a few seconds.

Carcioffi
CRUDI CON *Parmigiano*
ARTICHOKES WITH PARMIGIANO

3–4 artichokes

juice of 2 lemons

¾ cup olive oil

Maldon sea salt and freshly ground black pepper

piece of fresh parmigiano

If you can buy red artichokes with the thorns on the end of their leaves, they are ideal. Peel away the first few layers of leaves until you get to the tender ones.

Cut the top half of the artichokes away crosswise, then cut the stem part in half, lengthwise. Put in cold water with the juice of 1 lemon so that the artichokes don't go brown.

Mix remaining lemon juice, olive oil, salt and pepper and put this into a serving dish.

If the artichokes have a beard, cut that out very carefully and then slice them very finely. Dry slices on paper towels. Immediately put the artichoke slices in the lemon and olive oil sauce.

Now slice some parmigiano very thinly and add to the artichokes.

Serves 4-6

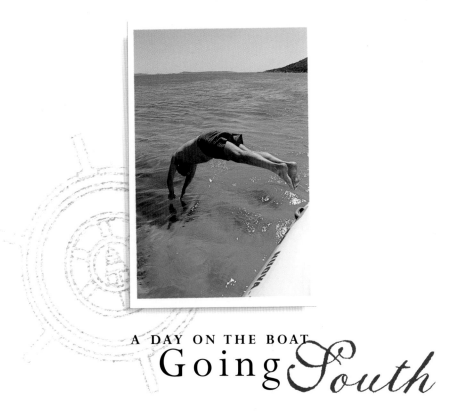

A DAY ON THE BOAT
Going *South*

THE WATERS OF THE COSTA SMERALDA ARE A BOATING PARADISE. THROUGHOUT the season boats of all sizes and sorts can be seen tied up in the ports, sailing or cruising the seas or anchored in sheltered bays, enjoying the sun and the clear and remarkably clean water.

The coast itself is rugged and rocky, mainly great granite boulders, smooth and weather-worn, tumbling into the sea. It is an indented coastline with points, bays, anchorages and hidden reefs. Off this wild coast, heading northwards across the Straits of Bonifacio and towards the southern coast of Corsica, is an archipelago of wild and fairly barren islands, some inhabited, some not. They and the seas around them are a summer playground.

Porto Cervo, the main port on the Costa Smeralda, has an active yacht club. Throughout the season there are special regattas attracting sailors from all over the world. There are regattas for maxis, Swan class yachts, America's Cup yachts and a famous fortnight for vintage yachts. We are here this summer during a race week for Admiral's Cup class boats and the cafés are full of serious sailors and their support teams, poring over their laptops looking at weather forecasts, GPS plots or digital photographs of sail settings. The whiff of ruthless competition is in the air.

Left: The marina at Porto Cervo.

Typically, the Mediterranean has good stiff breezes for yachting throughout much of the summer so it's a rare day when you don't see sails, white, high-tech beige, or the riotous colours of spinnakers scattered across a foam-flecked bay.

Then there are the motor boats. There are two marinas in Porto Cervo, one by the yacht club and one just inside the narrow entrance. Every evening there they are all lined up, stern to the wharf, one vessel bigger than the next. For a sheer display of exuberant consumption it would have few parallels. As these giant boats are moored tightly together, getting them in and out of port is quite an art. A team of helpers in Zodiacs are there to catch and throw lines, or act as bow thrusters to ease their great white charges into what seems an impossibly small slot. The helpers in their Zodiacs are the cowboys of the port, zipping across the surface of the water like dragonflies on a pond, hair streaming and arms waving. Chief among them is Domenico, a power in the land, because it is he who often determines where your boat ends up in the pecking order. Domenico receives a lot of considered attention from captains anxious to gain what the boat's owner sees as their rightful place in the world.

Once the yachts are secured tightly in their berths, the crews spring to action, hosing, cleaning and polishing away the salt of the day. In a ritual that seems compulsory, large, elaborate flower settings are carefully and conspicuously positioned on the rear decks next to the wharf. At a certain point in the evening the maritime version of the 'passegiata', the famous Italian pedestrian parade, begins with curious onlookers strolling the wharf to look at the boats while, on the spacious rear decks, the owners and their guests relax with their drinks around the flower settings and gaze at the passers-by without eye contact. This is the social theatre of the passegiata with a high-life twist.

When we are in Sardegna, we often rent a boat to enjoy the beauties of the coast and the offshore islands. Not, I hasten to say, one of the white giants, but usually a roomy Zodiac with a large motor that allows us to skim to our chosen spot and get out of trouble quickly if the wind changes or a storm approaches.

So now comes the big choice – do you go south or north out of the port? It usually depends on the wind, the sea and the weather forecast. We have decided to head south along the coast to some rocky islets a few kilometres off the coast. At a

Left: Lunch on the boat. Above: Looking back at the Costa Smeralda from the island of Mortoio.

Lunch on the boat – the art of the possible.

sheltered anchorage, their flat granite rocks slope into pristine water. We steer the boat along the coast between Porto Cervo and Cala di Volpe, passing the bay of Romazzino. This is a beautiful rocky coast with occasional beaches. It is also the best way to do a little villa spotting. The grand houses run down to the water with their white walls and manicured gardens and lawns. Hidden from curious passers-by on their inland side, they reveal all their splendour to the water. And some are very splendid indeed. In the early days of the Costa Smeralda, these giant villas perched on an isolated coastline echoed the palazzi on the wilder shores of Lake Como two hundred years earlier, when summer living fashions were different but the desire for comfort and grandeur was the same. The villas today are numerous although generously spaced and half-hidden from each other. Because of the strict building codes governing the Costa Smeralda, you don't see the blots on the landscape that litter less-controlled coastal areas. And, of course, the Italians do have a great sense of style, both in their houses and their boats.

Before going to the island, we decide to have a swim at Long Beach – a marvellous stretch of white sand at the entrance of the bay of Liscia Ruja which leads to the famous Cala di Volpe hotel.

On the beach, summer is in full swing. The style this summer, as it always seems to be, is minimum clothing, maximum tan. The beach is a smorgasbord of bodies and activity, including the mandatory day-long parade up and down at the water's edge. Threading their way through the bodies are North African traders in their long white jalabas, trading clothes, jewellery, premium-brand bags and other luxury goods, all at a fraction of the price of the same items in the elegant shopping colonnades of Porto Cervo.

The person next to us wants a 'Louis Vuitton' bag, but not one of the ones the trader is carrying. 'Come back tomorrow and I will have one for you.' Rumour has it, and Italians are always good for a conspiracy theory, that the factories in North Africa producing these goods are secretly part-owned by the big-brand companies themselves. They tried to stop the imitators, found they could not, so decided to join them instead. This is so outrageous it is obviously untrue. Or is it?

Having sampled the delights of Long Beach, we head out to the lugubriously named island of Mortoio (the graveyard). The island is uninhabited and no graves are in evidence, although on the maritime map it is marked as a restricted area. Being Italy, this seems to translate as 'It's restricted, it must be good, so let's go there'. On the way to Mortoio you look down the coast south to the imposing table mountain shape of Tavolara, its sheer sides plunging hundreds of metres into the sea. In a modest spot on the other side of Tavolara is the final resting place of

Garibaldi, the swashbuckling military leader who did so much to win the old Bourbon kingdom of the Two Sicilies for the new Italian state.

Safely anchored in a small bay surrounded by a devil's marbles of granite boulders lying half submerged in clean, sparkling water, we idle away the day sunbathing, swimming and generally lazing about.

Lunch on an open boat must, perforce, be simple. We carry an ice-box for drinks, salads and fruit. Lunch consists of crunchy ciabatta bread filled with whatever is on hand, but usually including mozzarella, ripe tomatoes dipped first in the sea, and Sardegnan pecorino cheese.

If you are feeling a little more ambitious, the thing to do is to prepare at home two or three simple plates that can be easily transported. My choices would be a frittata (the Italian omelette which is delicious eaten cold), a panzanella (a bread and tomato salad dressed with oil and vinegar) or a pan bagna – rolls filled with tomato, mozzarella and anchovies and drizzled with olive oil.

On the boat we follow lunch with fresh local fruit and perhaps some 'sospiri', literally 'sighs', a Sardegnan sweet made from sugar and marzipan.

Food on a boat is totally governed by the art of the possible. Even in a well-equipped galley the menu in a Force 6 gale is going to be very different from one at anchor in the shelter of port. In an open Zodiac, simplicity is of the essence. In that setting almost any food tastes quite marvellous.

After having had our fill of sun and salt water, we head back towards Porto Cervo. On the way, we have another swim stop at Pevero, a deep bay close to Porto Cervo and a favourite spot when the winds are blowing down from Corsica. The bay is scattered with boats at anchor like giant seagulls on the water. Summer in Sardegna is in full swing!

Nosing the boat into its berth in one of the small marinas, we tie up just as the first of the maxi boats start to return. It's time to go back to the house, shower, perhaps have a short siesta, then on to the evening's activities.

Pan *Bagna*

FILLED FRENCH BREAD

1 baguette (French stick), cut in half lengthwise

arugula (rocket)

anchovy fillets

pitted olives

very ripe tomato

VINAIGRETTE

¼ cup wine vinegar

½ cup virgin olive oil

1–2 teaspoons Dijon mustard

1–2 cloves garlic, crushed

salt and pepper

Make a vinaigrette dressing by mixing all ingredients. Put about 1–2 tablespoons of vinaigrette on each side of the baguette.

According to taste, put a few leaves of arugula (rocket) on each half, with a few anchovy fillets, a handful of pitted olives and a few slices of very ripe tomato.

Now wrap the baguette well in foil and leave in refrigerator for at least 2 hours or even overnight. All the flavours will penetrate the bread. You can put a weight on the baguette so that it is well pressed.

Variation

Fill baguette with grilled vegetables e.g. red or green capsicums (bell peppers) or eggplant (aubergine), some goats' cheese and a few rounds of red onion.

Panzanella

BREAD AND TOMATO SALAD

approx. 500 g (1 lb 2 oz)
old ciabatta bread

600 g (1 lb 5 oz) very ripe
tomatoes

2–3 cloves garlic, chopped

¼ cup red wine vinegar

1 chilli, chopped

10–15 leaves chopped basil

salt and pepper

½ cup virgin olive oil

*For this recipe you should use two-day-old
ciabatta bread.*

Cut bread into small cubes.

Put tomatoes in boiling water for 1–2 minutes,
drain and then peel. Chop finely.

Put all ingredients except oil in a bowl and mix well.
Squash mixture with your hands so it becomes a
paste. Then add some virgin olive oil – about ½ cup.

Leave in refrigerator for at least 1 hour.

Eat as antipasto.

Variation

*You can add a few chopped olives and chopped anchovy
fillets to the panzanella.*

Serves 4

Frittata
ITALIAN OMELETTE

12 organic eggs

¼ cup water

salt and freshly ground black pepper

2 heaped tablespoons grated parmigiano

2 large boiled potatoes, chopped

1 Spanish onion or 2 leeks, chopped

Beat eggs with a fork and add water, salt, pepper, parmigiano and chopped potatoes.

Fry onions or leeks in a little butter and oil until transparent and add to egg mixture. Put a little oil or butter in a non-stick frypan, pour in egg mixture and cook over medium heat for about 5 minutes. Then turn the grill (broiler) to medium and put the frittata under it. Grill for about 5 minutes or until the frittata is golden brown. Let cool and slide on to a serving dish.

Variation

You can use all sorts of vegetables to make frittata, e.g. asparagus, spinach or zucchini (courgettes). Very lightly cook the vegetables first.

Serves 6

Aperitivi

THE CURTAIN GOES UP

THERE ARE SOME THINGS IN LIFE THAT ARE DONE REGULARLY AND BECOME somewhat of a ritual. When we are in Sardegna the evening drinks – 'aperitivi' as they are called in Italian and it sounds better, more civilised – are such a ritual. Aperitivi are as much about where you are and what you do as what you drink. The word 'aperitivi' comes from the Italian word for open; a rough translation might be 'openers' and this is a good description. They are the curtain going up on an evening of social theatre.

The first decision is always, 'Where are we going to have aperitivi?' At Lu Nibaru the star attraction is the generous roof terrace from where you can look out over the bay of Liscia di Vacca, and see the sun dropping down over distant islands and mountains. It is a magical setting with a 360 degree view. We prepare a simple drinks tray with mineral waters, ice, lemons and a choice of the classic Italian aperitivi – Campari, Cynar, Martini Rosso or Punt e Mes. With these will be a bowl of local olives and some grissini, the thin Italian bread sticks or, my favourite, foglia di musica.

For some reason Italy has led the world in providing vermouth-style pre-dinner drinks. These are typically wine rather than spirit-based and all are flavoured with

Left: Aperitivi tray at Lu Nibaru.

unusual herbs and fragrances. Some are said to be based on cordials and special preparations that came out of the monasteries. Others were developed by entrepreneurs in the nineteenth century and are today part of the stock in trade of good bars all over the world. They represent one of Italy's rather unsung contributions to good living. As aperitivi in summer they are perfect.

For a different venue — more people, less nature — another choice is to have 'aperitivi in piazza', the village square in Porto Cervo. Here the action is usually in full swing as the evening passegiata of people streaming past to look or be looked at, flows in and around the square. The heavily tanned mix with the pale newly arrived, designer labels mix with the simple sarongs bought on the beach, the beautiful people mix with the very old, the very young and everyone in between. This is social theatre as an art form with everyone, whether walking and looking, or watching and commenting, joining in.

In the Porto Cervo passegiata a typical route is a leisurely stroll under the colonnades in the pedestrian-only street behind the piazza where every smart Italian designer seems to be represented. Mostly this is window shopping, but there are enough large logo-emblazoned carry-bags in evidence to suggest the shops are doing well. Following the shopping stroll, a walk through the piazza to see what's going on is essential, followed by a choice — at which bar will we have drinks?

In the Porto Cervo piazza there are three — one in front of the Porto Cervo hotel at one end of the piazza, one in the middle facing across the piazza to the port, and the third at the other end. Everyone has their pet likes and dislikes: in the 30 years we have been going to Sardegna I don't think I have ever drunk at the hotel bar, so it's a choice between the other two. The middle bar has the great advantage that it is on an elevated terrace giving a better view of the piazza and the boats beyond. It is attractively furnished with great pots filled with pomegranate trees and light summer furniture of pale turquoise. Last year we reluctantly had to avoid this bar in protest because a new operator had changed all the furniture to standard hotel brown. This year, we were delighted to see the turquoise furniture was back, the waiters smiling again. Apparently, we weren't the only people who thought the 'new' furniture was terrible.

Our favourite drink at this bar — the Bar del Portico, so called because of the colonnades at the back of the terrace with their low couches against the wall — is a Campari with fresh orange juice. The colour is extraordinary and the flavours are the scent of summer. Not everyone agrees; Jason, my 24-year-old son, thinks the Campari is better made with blood oranges, or better still, from pink grapefruit juice. The choice is yours!)

If we are not having aperitivi on the roof or in the piazza, then it's usually because we have been invited out to someone's house.

My cousin, Claudio Biaggi, has been going to Sardegna as long as we have. He, his wife Barbara and a succession of long, shaggy Skye terriers (the latest called Flynn) stay not far from us, but with a view looking the other way. From his terrace you can see the boats returning to Porto Cervo in a long procession that echoes the passegiata that is simultaneously in full swing at the piazza. Beyond the boats there is a marvellous view down the coast to the distinctive table-top profile of Tarolava.

Claudio and I are both grandchildren of my restaurateur grandfather, Ettore Biaggi. He resembles him in appearance and has always seemed to me to have inherited some of his artistic sensitivities about food and its settings. Aperitivi at Claudio's are always accompanied by a simple but tantalising array of bite-size pieces – pecorino cheese, diced tomatoes, two or three varieties of olives, grissini and other tasty offerings.

For an hour or so we sip our drinks, nibble, talk and savour the setting. This is a magic moment, the transition between the sun and the salt of the day and the cooler darkness of the Sardegnan night.

Then, as the curtain has risen on the evening, it is off to dinner at one of the many restaurants that the Costa Smeralda has to offer. Tonight we decide to go to a typically Sardegnan restaurant called Pietra Nieda.

Above: Aperitivi at Lu Nibaru on the rear terrace. My cousin Claudio, in the middle, is directing proceedings.

Mandorle

SPICED ALMONDS

2 tablespoons olive oil

2 cloves garlic, thinly sliced

6–8 sage leaves

1–2 sprigs of rosemary

250 g (9 oz) whole almonds

1 chilli, finely chopped
(optional, if you like it hot)

Maldon sea salt

In a saucepan heat olive oil, add garlic, fresh sage leaves and rosemary. Then put the almonds and chilli, if using, into the pan and sauté them until they start to brown. Pour off any extra olive oil, add Maldon salt and serve.

Variation

You can use other nuts instead of almonds.

Grissini Malfatti

ROUGH BREAD STICKS

1 quantity pizza dough
(see page 204)

olive oil

Maldon sea salt

Make the basic pizza dough.

Roll long little snakes, about 1 cm (½ in) thick and 30 cm (12 in) long. You can shape them the way you like, with little hooks at the end, or make a knot in the middle. Put them on a baking dish, brush them with olive oil, sprinkle with Maldon sea salt.

Bake in a hot oven (210°C/425°F) for a few minutes or until crisp.

Campari con *Pompelmo*

CAMPARI WITH GRAPEFRUIT JUICE

Campari

grapefruit juice

Mix Campari with freshly squeezed grapefruit juice – about one-third Campari to two-thirds juice – and add some ice. (If you have pink grapefruit, it looks even better.)

You can add 2–3 drops of Angostura bitters if desired.

Rossini

fresh raspberries

1-2 tablespoons fresh pineapple juice (optional)

sparkling white wine (champagne or Prosecco)

Crush the raspberries and pass them through a sieve. You can add fresh pineapple juice to the purée if the raspberries aren't sweet enough. Refrigerate until very cold.

Per bottle of champagne you will need 3 cups of raspberry purée. Mix them together in a jug and serve.

Bellini

fresh white peaches

sparkling white wine (champagne or Prosecco)

Use white peaches only. Mash them with a fork then pass them through a sieve. If they are not sweet, you can add a little sugar syrup.

You use 1 part peach purée to 3 parts champagne or Prosecco.

Tapanata

TAPENADE

**500 g (1 lb 2 oz) stoned
black or green olives (use
good quality olives!)**

2 cloves garlic

100 g (3½ oz) anchovy fillets

50 g (2 oz) capers

1 chilli

some fresh basil

**about 400 ml (13 fl oz)
virgin olive oil**

salt and pepper

Put all ingredients except oil, salt and pepper in mixer and blend, adding oil in a fine stream until you have the desired consistency. Taste and season with pepper and salt.

Acciugata
ANCHOVY DIP

300 g (10½ oz) anchovies

500 ml (1 pint) virgin olive oil

6 cloves garlic

2 teaspoons fresh thyme

3 teaspoons fresh basil

3 teaspoons Dijon mustard

3 teaspoons red wine vinegar

pepper

1 chilli

Put all ingredients in mixer and blend to a fine sauce.

Pâté
DI *Anguilla*
SMOKED EEL PÂTÉ

1 whole smoked eel,
about 450 g (1 lb)

125 g (4 oz) unsalted butter,
at room temperature

juice of 1 lemon

½ red onion, finely sliced

salt and pepper

Skin the eel and remove the backbone. Put flesh, broken in pieces, in the food processor with the butter, lemon juice and onion.

Process until it becomes a smooth mousse.

Taste and season with salt and pepper then refrigerate until needed.

Pietra Nieda
MAESTRO OF THE *Grill*

TRADITIONAL SARDEGNAN FOOD, AT LEAST IN THE GALLURA REGION IN THE north-east of the island, is not what we might expect of an island because it is based on meat dishes rather than fish. Life traditionally was centred inland around a few fertile valleys and rolling hillsides covered in low macchia scrub. A typical rural farmstead, or 'stazzu' as they are called, consisted of some small-scale low buildings around a yard. The family lived in one and the others were for storage or for animals. Grazing sheep was the mainstay of the local farming economy and a lot of Sardegnans worked as shepherds. From the sheep came a fairly coarse wool, meat and, of course, milk to make the famous pecorino – the sheep's milk cheese of the district – and a sheep's milk ricotta cheese. Also around the stazzu would be some pigs and the hillsides were full of wild boar.

So the grilling of meat, lamb or pork is at the heart of Sardegnans' traditional cooking – and they do it very well indeed. To experience the artistry of Sardegnan meat cooking, our favourite restaurant is Pietra Nieda (in Sardegnan dialect this means Black Rock). The restaurant is just off the main road heading to Cala di Volpe. You wind down a steep hill which has a panoramic view over the waters off Long Beach, the headlands beyond and Tavolara in the distance. As often as not there are

Left: Giovanni, head chef at Pietra Nieda, drizzling oil on grilled foglia di musica. Above: My son Jason enjoying malloreddu.

*Above: The garden
entrance and loggia
at Pietra Nieda.
Right: Dinner in
the spacious loggia
at Pietra Nieda.*

a few large yachts anchored in these sheltered waters, some because they are too big to get into the marina at Porto Cervo.

Apart from the cooking, the other welcoming characteristic of the restaurant is a large loggia room, open to the side with a view of hills and the distant sea. At the far end of the room, presiding over it in a culinary sense, is a long low masonry bench and, behind that, a chimney with a wide open cooking fire well equipped with spits, racks and skewers. This is the domain of the proprietor, Giovanni, a large, dark-haired man who is quiet and retiring to the point of shyness. What he has to say he says through his food and there is a ceaseless level of well-organised activity going on around the grill the whole evening. At one end of the grill you will see a baby suckling pig turning slowly on a spit as the house speciality, 'porcetta', gradually turns a golden brown. On the middle of the grill are spread lamb in racks or butterflied. Further to the left home-made spicy sausages are grilling together with the deep-purple of the radicchio leaves that will accompany them on the plate. A wedge of lemon, some salt and this simple dish is complete. The bitter taste of the radicchio and the acid of the lemon combine beautifully with grilled meat.

While Giovanni is quietly going about his business in the empire of the grill at

the end of the room, the front of house, Annino — his opposite in temperament, all smiles and warm welcomes — is seating his guests and engaging in long and passionate discussions on food choices. The whole engaging atmosphere is so Sardegnan we usually feel like ordering a Sardegnan pasta dish first, then the meat followed by, maybe, a sorbet, and the small elaborate Sardegnan biscuits called 'cuccindreddi' which they also do very well at Pietra Nieda.

We choose two dishes to start with. The first is Malloreddu, a Sardegnan version of gnocchi. The pasta needs to be individually rolled by patient hands to make each tiny 'dumpling'. It is the sort of work where traditionally you see, in a corner of the room, elderly grandmothers in black, their grey hair tied back in buns, patiently rolling away while surveying the room and chatting quietly amongst themselves. This is pretty much how they are made at Pietra Nieda. They come with a rich sauce made with a tomato base into which chunks of spicy sausage have been cut. It is a hearty peasant dish and it tastes marvellous.

The second dish we choose is Nudi — literally 'the naked', as it is like the inside of a ricotta and spinach ravioli without the outer pasta shell. The ricotta and spinach is lightly poached in small balls and is served with melted butter, sage and parmesan. It is lighter than ravioli and quite delicious.

We then decide to have grilled lamb and grilled purple radicchio leaves with lemon and salt. If you want to try something more special — an exceptional dish for a festive occasion — you should try the crowning glory of this sort of cooking, what I call Easter lamb. It takes eight hours to cook and originally would have been done in a wood-fired oven. For those who are passionate about being authentic, a pizza oven would be perfect. The lamb is cooked very slowly for about eight hours until, after you have been tortured all day by enticing aromas wafting from your oven, it is crisp all over, with the meat so soft it falls off the bone. It is the sort of dish that calls for a festive occasion and in many parts of the Mediterranean, including Sardegna, Easter is such an occasion. You choose the occasion, but at least once in their life everyone should try lamb cooked this way.

Eight -HOUR Lamb

1 baby, milk-fed lamb

1 whole bulb of garlic

fresh rosemary

¾ cup olive oil

2–3 teaspoons coarse salt

pepper

Ask the butcher to provide you with a milk-fed lamb. Also ask the butcher to remove the last 2 ribs so that you can fold the lamb into two.

Chop garlic and rosemary finely and add to olive oil and salt. Rub the lamb all over with this mixture. Preheat oven to 220°C (430°F). Put lamb on top of a wire rack in a deep oven pan and cook in oven for 10 minutes. Then turn the oven down to about 120°C (240°F). Let the lamb cook very slowly, basting it from time to time. All the fat will drip off the lamb and collect under the rack in the pan, leaving the lamb crispy.

Halfway through cooking (after 4 hours), turn the lamb upside down.

At the end of the cooking time the meat should fall off the bone and be all soft and crunchy at the same time.

Serve with a salsa verde (recipe page 148).

Serves 8–10 depending on size of lamb

Salsa *Verde*

GREEN SAUCE

1 bunch Italian parsley

1 handful mint leaves

6–8 anchovies

2 cloves garlic

juice of 1 lemon

2 teaspoons Dijon mustard

about 500 ml (1 pint)
virgin olive oil

salt and freshly ground
black pepper

Put all ingredients except oil into food processor. Process well then slowly add virgin olive oil. Taste for salt, add if necessary, and add ground pepper.

Malloreddu
CON RAGÙ DI *Salsiccia*

PASTA WITH SAUSAGE RAGU

500 g (1 lb 2 oz) malloreddu

RAGÙ DI SALSICCIA

1 red onion

2 cloves garlic

sage leaves, rosemary, 2 bay leaves – all fresh

6 thin slices lean pancetta

6 good quality pork sausages, sliced

½ glass dry red wine

600 g (1 lb 5 oz) peeled plum tomatoes

salt and freshly ground black pepper

Malloreddu is a dry pasta you can buy – it looks like little gnochetti.

Chop the onion, garlic, pancetta and add the herbs. Sauté in a little butter and olive oil until the onion turns transparent.

Add the sliced sausage, let it brown a bit, then add dry red wine. When the wine has evaporated, add the tomatoes. Cook for about 30 minutes. Taste for salt and pepper and season if necessary.

While sauce is cooking put a large pot of salted water on to boil and cook pasta until al dente. Serve pasta with sauce and freshly grated pecorino cheese.

Serves 4

Nudi

RICOTTA AND SPINACH GNOCCHI

1.2 kg (2½ lb) frozen spinach

500 g (1 lb 2 oz) ricotta

2 organic egg yolks

2 cups grated parmigiano plus extra 1 cup for table

salt and pepper

plain (all-purpose) flour, for dusting nudi

fresh sage leaves

100 g (3½ oz) unsalted butter

Squeeze all the water out of the spinach. Add to ricotta, egg yolks, parmigiano, salt and pepper and mix very well.

Take about 1 tablespoon of this mixture at a time and roll into little balls, dusting with flour.

Boil some salted water, and drop about 10 balls at a time into the water. As soon as they float to the surface, they are ready (about 1 minute). With a small sieve, fish them out and put them on a heated serving dish, one next to the other.

Put a generous sprinkling of parmigiano over the nudi.

Melt butter with sage, when it foams pour it over nudi, then serve immediately.

Serves 8

Cuccindreddi *E Tiliccas*

SARDENIAN ALMOND BISCUITS

PASTRY

100 g (3½ oz) butter
(traditionally suet was used)

500 g (1 lb 2 oz) unbleached
plain (all-purpose) flour
(see Note)

pinch of salt

FILLING

200 g (7 oz) ground almonds

200 g (7 oz) icing
(confectioner's) sugar

⅓ cup mirto liqueur

Preheat oven to 180°C (350°F).

Mix all pastry ingredients together then pass mix through pasta machine to make a thin long sheet (medium thin).

Mix all filling ingredients together well – it should be the consistency of marzipan.

Cut the pastry into strips about 10 cm (¼ in) wide, spread some filling in the middle, half close the strips lengthwise and then wind them round like a snake.

Put on a greased baking tray and bake in oven for about 20 minutes. They should still be pale in colour.

Note

Unbleached flour should be used, but best of all is Italian flour designed for pasta: farina Tipo '00'. Try speciality shops or Italian grocers and delicatessens.

Make 10-15 biscuits

Filetto di pesce persico.
Procuratevi 200 g. di filetto di pesc...
Lavatelo con cura e passatelo all'uo...
ed al pane grattugiato. Fatelo be...
rosolare da ambo le parti in u...
cucchiaino di burro. Dieci a 15 n...
di cottura. È consigliabile l'aggi...

Going North

TODAY THERE IS LITTLE WIND, THE FORECAST IS GOOD, SO WE DECIDE TO head north and see how far towards Corsica we can get.

The Straits of Bonifacio between Sardegna and Corsica have been, since time immemorial, a graveyard for hundreds of boats. The winds can be wild, and scattered in the middle of the straits are the islets of Cavallo and Lavezzi to trap the unseeing and the unwary. At Lavezzi there is a prominent monument to those who died in a calamitous shipwreck in Napoleon's time. Diving expeditions to view the wrecks near the islands are organised from the town of Bonifacio, which is perched on precipitous white cliffs that are visible miles away.

Bonifacio itself is a must-see. Too far to travel there safely in the Zodiac, it can be reached from Sardegna by ferries that regularly cross the straits. This old town is perched like a white piecrust on top of the cliffs, which drop 100 metres to the sea. The entrance to its port is a narrow gap in these cliffs, no more than 50 metres wide. In perilous times of old, chains were slung across the gap to stop raids by corsairs — or were the Bonifacians themselves the pirates and was this their lair? Probably both are true.

As times changed and public safety improved, the port sprang up on both sides

Left: Traditional Sardegnan fishing boats in the port at Maddalena. Above: Lighthouses mark a treacherous coastline. This one is at Capo Ferro.

Far right, top and middle: The port at Maddalena. Bottom: Yachts at anchor off the island of Budelli.

of a bay that is never more than 100 metres wide and runs inland for about a kilometre. It is a fabulous anchorage. Corsica is, of course, part of France, despite the efforts of some of its residents to have it otherwise. On a day trip you also cross the gastronomic border to Southern French food, leaving the prosciutto, parmigiano and mozzarella behind for the delights of omelette du jour and soupe de poisson.

Turning north out of Porto Cervo today, we head past the bay of Liscia di Vacca, where the house sits snug in its site almost invisible from the sea, and travel along the coast of the island of Caprera, then the island of Maddalena before heading out to the Marine National Park around the outer islands of Budelli, Spargi and Santa Maria.

The coasts of these outer islands are a marine wonderland of small bays, wild craggy shorelines, perfect white and pink sand beaches and stretches of the famous emerald water that gives the Costa Smeralda its name. Once threatened by being loved to death due to the pressure of visiting boats, the area is now part of a Marine National Park and is well controlled by rangers, who keep the larger boats out to sea and prevent smaller craft from parking on the beaches.

We have many favourite spots and it depends on the day where we go. Perhaps the most spectacular is the relatively shallow lagoon between the islands of Budelli and Santa Maria. Because it is shallow the white sandy sea bottom turns the water from Mediterranean blue to an expanse of almost tropical emerald. The lagoon has beautiful beaches and is full of nooks and crannies where a small boat can drop anchor and you can swim ashore.

On a day like this we like to go to a number of spots, have a swim and then move on. The possibilities are endless. Finally sated with sun and salt water, we head back, but the day is not over. It is a tradition on the way back to call in at Maddalena or Porto Rafael to have a coffee and an ice cream. Today, we decide we want to visit both places.

The old town on the island of Maddalena, sitting behind its small port, is everyone's idea of a romantic Mediterranean spot. The port is full of boats, including many of the area's traditional old wooden sailing boats. Next to the port is a square, where Garibaldi's statue prominently stands watch, and the town straggles along two streets above the waterfront. Here are many fine buildings, some quite elaborate in

Traditional architecture of the islands.

the classical manner. There is an imposing town hall, an elegant church and a generous waterfront piazza studded with handsome palms and eucalypts.

On the waterfront, where the big ferries come in from Palau on the main island of Sardegna, there are a slew of bars and pizzerie, many patronised by Italian and American sailors. Just across the waters from Maddalena is a big American naval base with all the support services for nuclear submarines. During the Cold War, this base was a key military asset. On occasions we have been on waters off Caprera when, all of a sudden, the sky would darken with helicopters and before long the huge black wedge of a conning tower would appear on the surface followed by the great length of the hull of the submarine. Even on the sunniest day the whole performance would have an air of unmistakable menace, the shadow of nuclear apocalypse.

Maddalena is a town that takes the siesta seriously. We arrive about 2 p.m. to find everything closed until 4 p.m., but we do manage to find an excellent coffee before heading across the waters to the tiny Porto Rafael and a gelato.

Porto Rafael is outside the Costa Smeralda but was developed about the same time and with similar strict controls. A wild rocky promontory sticks out towards

the island of Maddalena and provides good shelter in its lee side from the prevailing winds. Dotted inconspicuously among massive giant boulders are a number of smallish but very attractive villas. The centre of life around here is the little village square, which sits at the water's edge and is open on one side to the spectacular view. The other three sides of the square are occupied by small, low white-washed buildings, punctuated with the bright blues and greens of windows and shutters and the riotous purple of swathes of bougainvillea.

In the square there is a small café and two or three shops. The whole thing is as pretty as a picture with a faint air of a film set about it. Time has settled the square in its landscape and as the years go by it seems to become more part of things, more genuine.

The gelati are excellent. I have my usual hazelnut – there are times when I seem to be conducting an Italy-wide search for the best hazelnut ice cream – and the others like the sharpness of their lemon sorbets. It is an idyllic setting and the ice creams taste even better than usual with salt on your lips. After the ice creams and more coffees, we pile back into the boat for a fast run with a following wind back down the passage to Porto Cervo.

On an afternoon like this, gelati are very much on my mind so here is a collection of some of my favourites. They are all sorbets, lighter and more refreshing in summer than ice creams. Instead of traditional fruit sorbets they are made with some non-traditional fruits: blood orange, pineapple, raspberries and mango. They all have both taste and colour. Then I have included two flavours associated with ice creams rather than sorbets – coffee and chocolate. I think they are deliciously different, but you should make up your own mind.

Left: Buildings and laneways at Porto Rafael.

Sorbetto
DI *Sanguinelli*
BLOOD ORANGE SORBET

6–7 blood oranges

60 g (2 oz) caster (superfine) sugar

Juice all the oranges except one, which should be cut into pieces, skin and pips removed. Put orange flesh into food processor and process until smooth. Add the juice of remaining oranges and the sugar. Process for a few seconds. Taste to see if sweet enough and add more sugar if needed.

Put in ice-cream maker and churn until frozen — the sorbet should remain fluffy.

Serves 6

Sorbetto
AL *Ananas*
PINEAPPLE SORBET

1 large ripe pineapple, skinned and cored

60 g (2 oz) sugar

100 ml (3½ fl oz) water

Cut pineapple into pieces, put it in food processor and process until smooth.

Make a syrup with sugar and water and, when cool, add to pineapple purée. Taste to see if sweet enough and add more sugar if needed.

Churn in ice-cream maker until fluffy.

Variation

You can add 3–4 fresh mint leaves, chopped very finely before putting into ice-cream maker.

Serves 6

Sorbetto
DI *Lamponi*
RASPBERRY SORBET

600 g (1 lb 5 oz) raspberries
(frozen raspberries may be used)

juice of 1 lemon

50 g (2 oz) caster (superfine) sugar

Put everything into food processor and purée well.
Taste and, if needed, add more sugar or, if not enough
lemon, add more lemon juice. It should be quite tart
but not overwhelmingly lemony.
Put in ice-cream maker and churn until fluffy.
Tip
If you use frozen raspberries, put them frozen in the food
processor, add sugar and lemon and then process it all.
You will see you will get an instant frozen sorbet.
Serves 6

Sorbetto
DI *Mango*
MANGO SORBET

3 mangoes, skinned and stoned

2–3 tablespoons caster
(superfine) sugar (optional)

limoncello

You can use frozen mango halves if fresh fruit is not available.
Purée mangoes. If not sweet enough, add caster sugar.
Put into ice-cream maker and churn until light and fluffy.
Serve with a little limoncello poured over the sorbet.
Serves 6

Sorbetto DI *Caffè*

COFFEE SORBET

1 litre (2 pints) strong espresso coffee

280 g (10 oz) caster (superfine) sugar

1 tablespoon ground coffee

250 ml (8½ fl oz) cream, whipped (optional)

Dissolve sugar into hot coffee. Allow to cool then add the ground coffee. Put mix in the ice-cream maker and churn until light and fluffy.

Spoon into glass cups or glasses and serve with some softly whipped cream.

Serves 6

Sorbetto AL *Ciocolatto*

CHOCOLATE SORBET

1 litre (generous 2 pints) water

250 g (9 oz) caster (superfine) sugar

200 g (7 oz) cocoa powder

1 tablespoon ground coffee

½ cup crème de cacao (optional, see Variation)

250 ml (8 ½ fl oz) thick fresh cream (optional)

This sorbet has quite a strong chocolate taste. It is also delicious served with some fresh thick cream. To be successful it requires a very good quality bitter cocoa powder: look for Swiss or Belgian.

Bring water to boil and dissolve sugar in it.

Put the cocoa powder and ground coffee in a bowl, add a little of the hot syrup and mix to a thick paste. Then add the rest of the water. Taste for sweetness: adjust if necessary by adding more sugar. Allow to cool, put into ice-cream maker and churn.

Whip cream lightly and serve with the chocolate sorbet, if desired.

Variation

You can add the crème de cacao to the sorbet before it is frozen, or pour it over later, or both if you prefer!

Serves 6

NIGHT GARDEN IN A Rosemary *Vecchio Stazzu*

FROM THE SMALL SHOPPING CENTRE AT THE TOP OF THE HILL ABOVE LU NIBARU, the road winds down through a landscape of huge, smooth granite boulders to the intense blue waters of the bay. To the left of the road are the white-washed houses of what once was a 'vecchio stazzu', a low group of buildings that combine a homestead with barns and pens for stock. Fifty years ago they would have been the only structures in this wild landscape. Today the hillside is speckled with villas hidden behind stone walls and billows of garden plants.

Further down the road is the beautiful five-star Pitrizza Hotel, built right at the beginning of the Costa Smeralda project so that prospective buyers of the smart villas you see today had somewhere to stay when they came down to buy their land and build their houses. The walls of the Hotel Pitrizza are faced in stone, the individual rooms set into the hillside, the exposed part of the roof grassed over. In front of the hotel is a natural-form swimming pool the colour of the sea beyond with an 'infinity edge' on its outer side so that looking over the pool the water seems to join seamlessly with the waters of the bay beyond.

The vecchio stazzu on the hillside has been, since the start of the Costa Smeralda, the home of the Restaurant Rosemary and its guiding light, extrovert

Left: The garden at Rosemary with its view of wild coastline and the sea beyond.

Irish-born Susanne Aymé. In the 30 years we have been coming to the Costa Smeralda there has always been 'Rosemary'. It is at the end of our road so it is, in a sense, a neighbourhood restaurant.

The food is not particularly Italian, but a mix of summer dishes that are right for the place and climate. In the simple garden at the back, you are surrounded by the walls of the stazzu on three sides and a low wall on the fourth side over which you can look down on the long valley of boulders and fields towards the sea. At twilight on a summer's evening – when one usually arrives – the sun is setting over a silver sea and the mountains turn faintly pink before dissolving into the shadows of the night. In one corner of the garden is an old spreading fig tree and lanterns are strung out over the small space. At the opposite corner is an outdoor grill on which a young chef is always performing feats of culinary skill with fish or meat dishes. On a sideboard as you enter is an array of home-made tarts and flans to tempt you at the end of dinner. This garden and its view are one of the truly magical places and Susanne is a warm and generous host.

The staff at Rosemary – young, decorative and enthusiastic – are often English or Australian. The feel of the restaurant is international but, in the greatest compliment they can pay, it always seems full of Italians. At the front of the restaurant is a large and comfortable bar where the action seems to go on after dinner as well as before.

Susanne came to Sardegna, all those years ago, opened her restaurant and has stayed ever since. Unlike many who come and go with the summer season, she lives in Sardegna year round. Her house, not surprisingly, is in San Pantaleo, an old inland village, because she feels it is a real community with a year-round life – unlike some of the new areas on the coast which seem to die for six months of the year.

The night we went to Rosemary everything was as it should be. The wind dropped and as we went out to the garden, the sun was just about to dip into the sea. The aroma of grilling fish wafted lightly over the garden as we sat down at the table with a glass of chilled rosé from the Gallura region. It was all simple but utterly memorable.

If you were sitting outside in a garden like the one at Rosemary, when the sun is setting and the wine is chilled, what would you like to eat? Here's my choice …

I would start with a simple fish dish that can be done on the grill, ideally an outside wood or charcoal fire. I have chosen Spiedini di Pesce Spada, swordfish on a skewer. Swordfish has a firm white flesh that is ideal to grill. With it I serve a salsa verde (green sauce) made from a mixture of herbs with anchovies and olive oil.

My favourite accompaniment for the fish is an Iranian salad of rice and baby broad beans. Much of Iranian food is perfect for al fresco living and serving it

Dinner in the garden at Rosemary.

reminds me of the early childhood years I spent in the exotic world outside Tehran.

And now the simplest of dishes, but the essence of summer, I serve Pomodorini al Forno – tomatoes baked in the oven with olive oil and garlic and sprinkled with salt. They look extraordinary and taste just as good.

To finish off, as they do at Rosemary, I would serve a Crostata di Datteri, a date tart. Dates are rich and sweet and seem right for this part of the Mediterranean. After all, you are only just across the water from North Africa, where they are a staple part of life. They also remind me of my childhood in Tehran.

Spiedini

DI PESCE *Spada*

SWORDFISH KEBABS

approx. 1 kg (2 lb 3 oz)
swordfish, cut in 2.5 cm
(1 in) cubes

fresh bay leaves

MARINADE

2 cloves garlic

1 chilli

Maldon sea salt

juice of ½ lemon

1 cup virgin olive oil

String fish cubes on wooden or steel skewers (if using wooden skewers, soak them first in water, so that they will not burn on the grill). After every third fish cube add a fresh bay leaf on the skewer.

In a mortar, mix all marinade ingredients together well. Pour this marinade over fish skewers and let rest for about 15 minutes.

Grill the fish on a very hot grill for about 3–4 minutes, turning the skewers from side to side so that the fish is nicely coloured all over. Serve with Salsa Verde with coriander and dill (see recipe page 174).

Serves 6

Polo
BA Bâghâli
IRANIAN RICE WITH BROAD BEANS

500 g (1 lb 2 oz) basmati rice

3–4 sprigs fresh coriander (cilantro)

3–4 sprigs fresh Italian parsley

3–4 sprigs fresh dill

3–4 fresh chives

500 g (1 lb 2 oz) fresh, shelled broad beans (if fresh ones are not available, use frozen)

100 g (3½ oz) butter

Put the broad beans in boiling water for 1 minute and then pop them out of their skins – which is a bit of a pain, but well worth it. Chop the fresh herbs very finely

Soak the rice in water, rinsing several times. Bring some salted water to the boil in a large saucepan. Pour in the rice and cook for about 10 minutes. It should still be slightly undercooked.

Now add the shelled broad beans and chopped herbs to the parboiled rice. Stir well so that they are mixed thoroughly, then drain at once. The herbs will cling to the rice.

In a saucepan melt butter, add rice and stir well; taste and add more salt if needed. Cover with a tight-fitting lid, and put on very low heat for a few minutes. Turn off the heat and let stand for another 15 minutes.

Serves 6

Pomodorini
AL *Forno*

BAKED TOMATOES

20–25 very ripe, vine-ripened
little tomatoes

2 tablespoons virgin olive oil

10 basil leaves

1 teaspoon fresh thyme

Maldon sea salt

3–4 garlic cloves, sliced

pepper

In an ovenproof dish, put some virgin olive oil, then add the tomatoes still attached to their stalks, some basil and fresh thyme, Maldon sea salt, 3–4 sliced garlic cloves and pepper.

Put in 220°C (430°F) oven for about 15–20 minutes.

Serves 4

Salsa *Verde*

WITH CORIANDER AND DILL

1 small bunch Italian parsley

½ bunch coriander (cilantro)

½ bunch dill

1 teaspoon Dijon mustard

juice of 1 lemon

1 chilli (optional)

1 egg yolk

1 cup virgin olive oil

salt and freshly
ground black pepper

Because I want to serve the swordfish with the Iranian rice, which is made with fresh herbs, including dill and coriander — both strong flavours — I will add these two to my salsa verde.

Place all ingredients except oil and seasoning in food processor, and mix very well. Then add oil very slowly, as if you were making mayonnaise. The salsa verde should be quite thick in consistency. Add salt and pepper to taste.

Crostata

DI *Datteri*

DATE TART

PASTRY

125 g (4 oz) unsalted butter

200 g (7 oz) plain (all-purpose) flour

60 g (2 oz) sugar

pinch of salt

rind of 1 lemon and few drops of juice

FILLING

125 g (4 oz) unsalted butter

125 g (4 oz) coconut cream

½ cup brown sugar

pinch of salt

¼ cup nocino (walnut liqueur), or mirto liqueur (optional)

approx. 30 dates cut lengthwise, stones removed

Process all pastry ingredients in food processor.
Roll out and lay in a 28 cm (11 in) springform pan.
Put in freezer for about 30 minutes.

Preheat oven to 200°C (400°F). Take pastry from freezer; prick base then blind bake pastry in oven until lightly coloured – about 15 minutes.

Mix all filling ingredients, except dates, and boil on top of stove for 20 minutes. Let cool.

When pastry is cool, put dates in fan shape on top of pastry. Pour the cooled sauce over the dates (if the sauce is too hot, it will be too liquid and soften the pastry).

Serve with whipped cream.

Serves 8

San Pantaleo

AND THE MOUNTAINS OF THE

Seven Sisters

IF YOU DRIVE INLAND, AWAY FROM THE COSTA SMERALDA, THERE IS A POINT where the road passes the crest of a hill and you gaze down a long valley, its floor a patchwork of fields and stone walls, its rolling hillsides covered in low bushes and trees. In the distance is a range of impossibly wild granite mountains, the tallest of which is crowned by seven jagged crags, remnants of some heroic geological event in the not-too-distant past. Anywhere else this formidable range would have some daunting name like 'Crown of Thorns' or the 'Devil's Jawbone'. Here it is called – for reasons lost in the mists of local legend – the 'Mountains of the Seven Sisters'.

When we are in Sardegna we go to these mountains often because, nestling on the small plateau at their base, with a commanding view of the countryside and the valley below, is the old village of San Pantaleo. When you drive up the winding road from the valley you reach the plateau and then turn off and park to walk to a piazza that is picture-perfect.

It is not the grand piazza of Italian mainland cities with their vast scale and ornate Palladian façades. San Pantaleo, until recently, was a poor mountain village. The houses are low and small, with no elaboration on their frontages whatsoever. They are the simple structures of the stazzu, ordered around three sides of a square

Left: The village square of San Pantaleo, with its flowering standard oleanders.
Above: Ristorante da Tito, with the Mountains of the Seven Sisters on the skyline behind.

The caffè in the square,
San Pantaleo.

that is about 50 metres wide and 80 metres long. On the fourth side is the old stone façade of a beautiful small church, fairly elaborate for this village, but by the standards of Italian ecclesiastical architecture it is austerity itself. On either side of the square, stretching from one end to the other, are two rows of very old oleanders, pruned to be standard with thick bare trunks and moppy tops. In summer these are a cloud of white flowers that persist for weeks. In this way the simplest of settings is dressed with a festive air.

There is a market in the piazza on Tuesdays and the square then fills with small stalls selling local handicrafts (particularly the fine Sardegnan embroidered cloth), carpets and foods. We usually go in the evening when the market has packed up, to drink 'aperitivi' at a small café with two or three tables outside on the pavement at the end of the piazza opposite the church.

The passegiata San Pantaleo-style is in full swing. This is quite different from the glitter and buzz of Porto Cervo. You usually see a group of the 'local lads' leaning casually on their motor bikes, some younger passers-by with children and a few old, very weather-beaten men sitting and watching. The old men, probably shepherds in

their day, would have grown up poor and had a hard working life. They clearly enjoy these softer times, but you sense an element of disbelief. If you really want to engage their interest and attention, you have to be able to talk about their lifetime interest – sheep. It's no different from parts of the countryside in Australia in that regard.

After a drink in the piazza we move on to one of the restaurants we most enjoy in Sardegna. 'Da Tito' is presided over by the friendly lord of the manor, Tito himself. The establishment is a small hotel with guest rooms above and, on the ground floor, a long dining room, almost the full length of the building; along its outside wall is a generous loggia of the same length. The loggia is where you want to sit, gazing through its open side to the fruit trees and the valley beyond. Behind, glimpsed from the end of the room, is the granite ridge line leading to the Mountains of the Seven Sisters.

Tito is a warm and attentive host. There is no menu as such, but he guides you through the evening's culinary offerings, each plate sounding more desirable than the next.

Village houses,
San Pantaleo.

At da Tito there is only one place to start and that is a magnificent table along one wall of the dining room that is completely covered with plates of various delicacies — it really is a 'grand antipasto'. There are mussels, octopus, raw salads of zucchini and cauliflower, eggplant, frittata, prawns, anchovies, herrings, olives, peppers and much much more. So the first course of the evening is always the antipasto.

For the hungry there are interesting pasta dishes, but I hold back because I know what is coming next, Tito's famous Pesce al Sale, a whole fish baked in a crust of salt. The salt seals in all the juices of the fish as it cooks but, perhaps surprisingly, it does not make the fish itself taste salty. The taste is subtle and moist with all the flavours of the sea — and it is a piece of gastronomic bravado as the salt-encrusted fish is opened at the table.

To follow, like the antipasto, there are lots of choices, but really only one — home-made rice ice cream with Tito's own raisin sauce called 'saba', made from the must of wine pressings. Try as I might, I have not been able to replicate Tito's saba — he has been helpful, but did he 'inadvertently' leave something out? With something as special as this you would be tempted not to share it with the world. But it is an ambition of mine to make a saba like Tito's and, when I do, I will tell you about it and the rice ice cream that goes with it.

What I can do is give you the recipes for the things I would put on my plate from the antipasto. These are all dishes that are suitable for a wide number of occasions. They are good for lunch, sometimes alone or just a couple of them, they are a great first course at dinner and, in combination, as a grand antipasto they are a veritable feast.

I have also included my recipe for Pesce al Sale, a marvellous dish for a special occasion.

Antipasto DI Cozze

GRILLED MUSSELS

FOR ABOUT 4 PEOPLE USE:

1 kg (2 lb 3 oz) mussels

2 cloves garlic, chopped

1 handful finely chopped
Italian parsley

¾ cup breadcrumbs

⅓ cup olive oil

freshly ground black pepper
and salt

The quantities depend a bit on whether you want to make this dish as part of an antipasto or to serve it as a main antipasto. As a main antipasto calculate about 6–8 mussels per person.

Clean the mussels under running cold water and pull or cut away their beards.

Put about ½ cup of water in a large saucepan and heat; when it boils add the mussels, cover the pan and let them cook until the shells open. Shake the pan from time to time – mussels will take about 5 minutes to open.

When they are cool enough to handle, arrange them on an ovenproof dish, using only one half of the shell. Turn on grill (broiler) to preheat.

In a bowl mix breadcrumbs, garlic, parsley, olive oil, salt and pepper and mix to a crumbly paste. Now put on every half-shell a bit of this mixture, pressing down well around the mussel. Put under hot grill for only a few minutes until topping starts to colour but not burn.

Can be eaten hot or cold.

Acciughe *Fresche*

FRESH ANCHOVIES

8–16 fresh anchovies
½ cup breadcrumbs
1–2 cloves garlic, crushed
1 chilli, finely chopped
1 handful finely chopped
Italian parsley
salt and freshly ground
black pepper
olive oil

Calculate about 2–3 fresh anchovies per person if this dish is part of an antipasto, or 4 per person if it is served as a first course.

Preheat oven to 220°C (430°F).

Split open the fresh anchovies down the belly, then remove heads and spines. Wash under running water and dry with paper towels. Put fish flat, belly side down and spread open on paper towels.

Put the breadcrumbs, garlic, chilli, parsley, salt and pepper in a bowl. Mix with a spoon.

Oil an ovenproof serving dish, sprinkle some of the breadcrumb mixture evenly but not too thickly on the bottom of the dish. Arrange the anchovies, one next to the other open on the dish. Sprinkle some more breadcrumb mix on top and then sprinkle some olive oil all over the fish.

Put in oven for about 5 minutes. The fish should just take a little bit of colour.

The anchovies can be eaten hot or cold.

Peperoni  con *Acciughe*

CAPSICUM WITH ANCHOVIES

3 firm red peppers (bell capsicums)

1 firm yellow pepper (bell capsicum)

2–3 cloves garlic

fresh basil

15 anchovies

virgin olive oil

Blacken the skin of the peppers over a flame, turning the peppers over and over (tongs are the best implement for this); when black put in a plastic bag, let stand for a few minutes. The skin will then just slide off. The flesh of the peppers should still be firm, not mushy.

Cut the peppers in slices, removing cores and seeds, and dry them well with paper towels. Remove any remaining pieces of skin.

In a serving dish arrange a layer of peppers then some chopped garlic, basil and some anchovy fillets. Continue layering until everything is used up.

Now cover with virgin olive oil and let stand for a few hours before serving.

Serves 6

Polipi con Patate

OCTOPUS WITH POTATOES

3–4 medium octopus

2 lemons

2–3 fresh bay leaves

1 kg (2 lb 3 oz) yellow waxy potatoes, e.g. kipfler

lemon juice

1 cup virgin olive oil

salt and freshly ground black pepper

Italian parsley, finely chopped

Cut the heads off the octopus and discard.

Bring some water to the boil, add ½ lemon, sliced, and bay leaves. Add the octopus and boil for about 20 minutes. Allow to cool in the water.

Boil the potatoes and when cooked cut them into bite-sized pieces.

Pull off the octopus legs, remove the slimy skin and cut flesh into bite-sized pieces. Add to potatoes.

Mix juice of remaining 1½ lemons, olive oil, salt, pepper and parsley together well. Pour over octopus and potatoes.

The octopus should be eaten at room temperature.

Serves 6

Gamberetti con *Ruggola*

PRAWNS WITH ARUGULA

600 g (1 lb 5 oz)
small prawns (shrimp)

juice of 1 lemon

½– ¾ cup virgin olive oil

salt and pepper

1 bunch baby arugula (rocket)

If you can get the very small, green, fresh school prawns (shrimp), they are great!

Boil some water and salt. As soon as it boils, throw in the green prawns and when water comes back to the boil and the prawns have turned pink, drain and refresh them in cold water to prevent further cooking.

Shell prawns. It is a bit of a labour of love, but well worth it!

Beat lemon juice, oil, salt and pepper in a bowl and add the prawns. Toss the arugula with the prawns and eat immediately, otherwise the leaves become black and limp.

Serves 4

Pesce

AL *Sale con Olio e Limone*

FISH IN A SALT CRUST WITH A LEMON AND OIL DRESSING

1 whole fish (about 1½–2 kg/3½–4½ lb) – gutted and cleaned inside but with scales on

lemon slices

fennel, sliced or bay leaves, tarragon or thyme

approx. 2 kg (4 lb 6 oz) salt – any type, fine or coarse, but fine salt sticks better

½ cup plain (all-purpose) flour

water

DRESSING

juice of 1 lemon

¾ cup virgin olive oil

My favourite fish for this dish is red emperor, but you can use snapper or any firm white-fleshed fish.

Preheat oven to 200°C (400°F). Put fish in an oiled baking dish and in its stomach cavity put some lemon and fennel slices (or fresh herbs).

In a bowl mix the salt with the flour and enough water to make a dry paste.

Cover the fish thickly with the salt, making sure it is well sealed everywhere (see Note). Bake in the oven for about 40 minutes.

Break the salt crust at the table, in front of your guests, as it looks impressive. Make sure you remove all the salt crust. Usually the skin of the fish will come off easily with the crust.

Mix fresh lemon juice and virgin olive oil and serve as a dressing.

Note

If the fish is large, you can leave the head without salt, so that you have enough to cover the body properly.

Serves 6

Tenuta
DI *Capichera*

SARDEGNAN WINES, PARTICULARLY THOSE FROM THE GALLURA REGION IN
the north-east of the island, inland and north of the Costa Smeralda, have always
been known as good everyday drinking wines. (Gallura was for centuries fairly
isolated and even had its own language, unintelligible to Italian speakers.) In
particular, the whites and the rosés are often seen on the tables of the summer
visitors, and rightly so. They are fresh, simple wines that go well with the food and
the climate.

All that has begun to change. One night at da Tito in San Pantaleo, Tito
recommended a marvellous white wine from a vineyard not far away. It was made
from vermentina grapes and had been well-aged in oak barrels to produce an
exceptional wine of character and complexity. It turned out that Tito knew the
family who owned the vineyard well – that was how he was able to get a supply of
the wine, as it was in great demand.

A few days later, he arranged for us to visit the vineyard, the Tenuta di
Capichera. With Tito we drove from San Pantaleo through sun-bleached fields,
bordered with stone walls, along roads often lined with eucalyptus trees and the
low, scented shrubs of the Sardegnan hinterland. Leaving the road, we followed a

new unsealed track through a wild valley until we saw, from a bend, a handsome new winery of impressive proportions. On the top of the hill the winery had a commanding view of the rolling hillsides of the Tenuta di Capichera.

Mario Ragnedda, a son of the family who owns the business, showed us around. Mario's family have been growing grapes here for over 100 years; the land belonged to his grandfather, then to his mother. The big change came about 25 years ago when Mario's father, Alberto Ragnedda, began replanting vermentina grapes and introducing modern wine-making techniques. He set out to make a great white wine from the vermentina variety.

It was a radical idea, greeted at the time with a great deal of scepticism. Today the wine is known and appreciated all over Italy. Some 200,000 bottles are produced a year, from 300 hectares of vines, and it typically sells for about five times the price of ordinary vermentina wine. Single-handedly the Ragnedda family have pioneered quality wine-making in Sardegna. Fabrizio, Mario's brother, who is the wine-maker, has in fact invented quality Sardegnan white wine and where the Ragneddas blazed the trail, others have now followed.

It probably helped that these advances in wine-making were being made just at the time when visitors started to pour into the new summer resort of the Costa Smeralda. Tasting the local wines and liking what they drank they continued to request the wine when they returned home. The reputation of vermentina soared and today, according to Mario, it is the most requested variety in Italy.

Fabrizio was away in Argentina looking for skilled workers for the winery and Mario explained that Sardegnans preferred the new jobs in hotels, bars and shops and were not keen on the hard work in the hot sun that grape tending and picking involved. Sardegnans who had emigrated to find their fortune in the New World were now being tempted back to take jobs the people they left behind no longer wanted. It was a measure of how far this once impoverished region has come over the last 30 years.

Later we drove through the manicured hillsides of immaculately tended vines to a special place, something of a sacred site, called 'tomba dei giganti', or tombstone of the giants. There we found an ancient carved monolith in a distinctive shape sited, Mario told us, on an underground river of water and energy. The tomba dei giganti monolith is famous in Capichera, so it is fitting that it is the emblem on the labels of some of their wines.

Sardegna has many prehistoric stone structures, tombs, mounds and old fortifications, called collectively 'nuraghi'. It is known they are very ancient but not a lot else is known, other than in local legend, about their origins and the people who built them. They are reminders that this island has been inhabited since the earliest times of Mediterranean settlement.

From Capichera we drove with Mario and Tito to the rich valley that runs inland from the northern town of Palau, the staging point for the ferry to go to the island of Maddalena. At one time the valley was full of small vineyards. Now there are very few, as the allure of the towns sucks the young people of the old farming families away from the land. On one such piece of land Alberto and his family are re-establishing a substantial vineyard. From this hillside, with young vines streaming in lines down the valley, you can see in the distance the sparkle of intense blue that is the sea.

Back at the winery we enjoy a tasting of Capichera wines. The vermentina we had drunk and enjoyed at Tito's, so Mario opens some bottles of new red wines where the family is also pioneering quality wine-making. The wines are made from a single grape variety, cariniamo – always a most demanding way to make a great wine. The wines are young and made to be aged, but already they are showing great individuality and promise of distinction. Mario says people either love them or hate them, but only time will tell whether this new initiative of the Tenuta di Capichera will also command a great reputation. Given what they have achieved with vermentina, it would be a brave person to claim that the Ragnedda family could not do it again.

All this trekking around the hilly vineyards in the hot sun has made us think of lunch. What would go well with the cold bottle of Vermentina di Tenuta di Capichera in the fridge back at the house?

I decide on a light summer lunch of tuna with two different bean salads. The tuna is made from fresh fish cooked and preserved under oil. Once you have made it, it is there in the fridge to be eaten at short notice – a delicious alternative to the classic tinned tuna used in Italian cooking.

One bean salad is made with borlotti beans, the other with the white cannellini beans. Both are simple, fine tasting and are an excellent accompaniment to the tuna. With a cold glass of the Tenuta di Capichera vermentina complementing the meal, life is looking good.

Far left, top: Wine aging in casks in the cellars of Tenuta di Capichera. Far left, bottom: Tito with Mario Ragnedda. Above, top: Roadside sign to the vineyard. Above, bottom: Tomba dei Giganti.

Tonno
Pott'Olio
TUNA IN OIL

1 piece of fresh tuna, about 1 kg
(2 lb 3 oz)

1 litre (34 fl oz) olive oil

200 ml (7 fl oz) grape seed oil
(see Note)

4–5 fresh bay leaves

fresh thyme

whole peppercorns

1–2 chillies

COURT BOUILLON

1–2 celery sticks and leaves, cut
in pieces

1–2 cloves garlic

3 cloves

1 large onion, cut into pieces

1 teaspoon whole peppercorns

3–4 teaspoons salt

Put all bouillon ingredients in about 2 litres (5 pints)
of water and boil for about 30 minutes, to release all
the flavours. Now add the tuna to the cooked bouillon
and cook for about 15 minutes on low heat. Timing
depends a bit on the thickness of the piece of tuna:
it has to be only just cooked.

Let the tuna cool in the court bouillon for about
3 hours. Take it out, remove the skin and dry well
with paper towels.

Put the tuna in a glass jar or dish, cover with virgin
olive oil and grape seed oil plus the bay leaves, fresh
thyme, peppercorns and chillies.

Put in refrigerator for 48 hours before use.

Note

*The grape seed oil is essential, as it prevents the olive
oil solidifying when the tuna is kept in the fridge.*

Insalata
DI *Fagioli*
BORLOTTI BEAN SALAD

70 g (2½ oz) fresh beans per
serve, or 50 g (2 oz) dried beans

water

3 tablespoons virgin olive oil

Maldon sea salt and pepper

2 handfuls arugula
(rocket), chopped

*This recipe is best made with fresh borlotti beans,
if you can find them; otherwise soak dried beans
overnight, or at least for 6–8 hours, before use.*

Put some water and 1 tablespoon of oil to boil.
Do not add salt to water as it makes the skin of
beans go hard; the oil will soften the skin. Pour
in the beans and cook until tender, but not mushy –
about 20 minutes.

Drain and add 2 tablespoons virgin olive oil, Maldon
salt, pepper and, when the beans are cool, some finely
chopped arugula (rocket).

Serves 4

Insalata
DI *Canelli*

CANNELLINI BEAN SALAD

200–250 g (7–8½ oz) of dried cannellini beans

1 tablespoon virgin olive oil

3 cloves garlic

2–3 bay leaves (or sage leaves)

pinch of salt

1 chilli, chopped

1 handful of Italian parsley, chopped

oregano leaves

Soak beans overnight, or for at least 6 hours.

Boil beans in water with 1 tablespoon oil, 3 cloves garlic and 2–3 bay or sage leaves added. Cook until beans are tender but still have a bit of a bite – about 30 minutes.

Strain beans, discard herbs. Now crush the soft garlic with salt and chilli, mix with some chopped Italian parsley and a few fresh oregano leaves.

Mix back into beans.

Add some virgin olive oil and taste for seasoning.

Serves 4

Pazza
FOR
Pizza

ONE OF THE GREAT PLEASURES OF EATING IN ITALY IS THAT YOU CAN ALWAYS find a pizza. The Italians took flour, yeast, water, cheese and tomato and created the pizza. The English took the same ingredients and made a sandwich. Both are popular and capable of as much variation as your imagination allows – but I know which I prefer.

Pizza as we know it today was a dish that came out of the cucina povera of Naples. The classic Neopolitan pizza is the Margherita, named after a queen who, given that it was the food of common people, probably never ate one. Whoever named it after her was either out to curry a little royal favour or, more likely, thought it was good marketing to associate the product with the royal name. Pizza Margherita – tomato, mozzarella cheese, oil and basil – is one of the great signature dishes of modern eating. Like a villa by Palladio, it has spawned countless imitations, variations and bastardisations that are to be found somewhere in every town square in the Western world. If you go to Naples today, you will find they still serve pizza Margherita in preference to all others, for its refined perfection.

And, of course, the pizza is great for al fresco eating.

In Sardegna when we feel like pizza we go to Il Baretto, which is a relaxed

Pizza making can be a family affair. Here my daughter Miranda prepares the dough.

pizzeria with an enormous open terrace, a long loggia and large inside rooms for cold nights. Crossing the terrace, passing under the loggia, you walk in the door and there it is — a huge wood-fired oven with two or three toiling 'pizzaioli', pizza-makers, feeding it with the creations they have prepared on a long bench.

Il Baretto is a little unusual for Sardegna. Just down the road from the smart hotel Cala di Volpe, it is very relaxed and casual. Young families are there with their children who are playing on the slides and swings nearby, boaties are there in their shorts and singlets, and staff from the smart restaurants go there on their days off. This is how we first heard about it, from Silverio at the Bar del Porto, a waiter who was a fund of knowledge on all things Sardegnan, including the bandit stories of old.

With dinner at Il Baretto, pizza is the main event. As a first course they recommend a varied and simple antipasto of local cheeses, olives, prosciutto and salami and various vegetables, grilled and sotto aceti (preserved in vinegar). With two large plates shared around the table and some Gallurese wine, it's a great start to the evening.

For the pizza itself — and Il Baretto has an extensive list — it's a matter of personal taste. I prefer one with simple ingredients. The crust has to be just right, which for me means thin. The topping has to be in proportion: three parts topping to one part crust might sound attractive, but it's just too much of a good thing. And the best pizzas are cooked in wood-fired ovens where the base acquires a little of the smoky aromas of the wood.

To be a good pizzaiolo is as much an art as a science. The fire has to be just right, the dough, the thickness of the crust, the choice of toppings and the way they are spread on the dough — all these have to be combined in exactly the right mix. When they are, a pizza is sublime — the gastronomic equivalent of the moment when a soprano shatters crystal with one pure note.

Pizza-making has a particular significance in my family. It has assumed the status of a tradition where the process — making the dough, tending the fire, preparing the pizzas — is as important as the end result. Everyone joins in somewhere and everyone has strong views on what they want on their pizza, often making it themselves.

It all started 23 years ago when my husband, young daughter, Miranda, and I were living in Milano. At the weekend we would go to Kailas, the family home in Lugano, for a change of pace and scenery. My uncle, Zio Camillo, was living in the house next door, where Luca now lives. Zio Camillo was a very good cook and among many other things he taught me to make pizza. Every Sunday I would go to his house after breakfast and we would make the dough, which would then be allowed to sit and rise for a few hours. Towards lunchtime, we would make the pizzas, put them in the oven and then serve them to the keenly awaiting family. Sunday lunch pizza became our tradition.

So it was natural, when living in Australia, that I continued the tradition, always dreaming I would one day have my own pizza oven. Well, now I have one. It is in the large veranda room of our beach house and pizza-making as well as pizza-eating has continued to be a family tradition.

Over time, after quite a lot of experimenting with various toppings, I have developed a repertoire of favourites. I always make a Margarita and it is always popular. I like very much some of the pizze biance, or white pizzas. In fact, long ago, before the tomato arrived in Italy from Peru, all pizza was pizza bianca. The simplest way is to baste the pizza crust with oil, salt, rosemary and maybe some black olives. The pizza bianca with potatoes is an unlikely combination, but it is really delicious. An unusual choice that always goes down well (the test is whether anything is left on the tray) is made with fresh leaves of arugula (rocket).

These are fairly traditional, but the variations are only limited by your imagination and what your taste buds tell you. Here are some suggestions to tempt you.

Manuela the pizzaiola –
at work at my pizza oven.

Pizza *Dough*

1 kg (2 lb 3 oz) plain
(all-purpose) flour, if possible
Tipo 'OO' (see Note), sifted

15 g (½ oz) salt

15 g (½ oz) granulated yeast

2 tablespoons virgin olive oil

2½–3 cups warm water

Mix all together well and then knead until the dough becomes shiny and elastic. Shape into a ball, put in a bowl and put a few drops of oil over the dough so that it does not dry out. Cover with cloth and let stand in a warm spot for about 1½ hours. Punch the dough down, knead again well and, if you have time, let it rise again.

Note

Unbleached flour should be used, but best of all is Italian flour designed for pasta: farina Tipo 'OO'. Try speciality shops or Italian grocers and delicatessens.

Makes about 4 pizzas on 30 x 40 cm (12 x 16 in) trays

Pizza *Bianca*
WHITE PIZZA

1 quantity pizza dough
(see above)

2–3 leeks, finely chopped

2–3 potatoes, sliced paper-thin

Maldon sea salt, freshly
ground black pepper

olive oil

fresh rosemary

Preheat oven to 240°C (460°F).

Cook the leeks in a little butter and olive oil until soft and sweet. Take a piece of dough (about 150–200 g/5–7 oz), flatten it until it is about 1 cm (½ in) thick and put it on an oiled oven tray. Spread the cooked leeks evenly over the dough and then arrange the potatoes like fish scales all over the pizza.

Sprinkle some Maldon salt and pepper on top, then drizzle olive oil all over the pizza, with some rosemary. Cook in oven for about 10–15 minutes or until the base is golden brown and crunchy.

Tip

If you have a pizza oven, it will only take 5 minutes to cook, so you should boil the potatoes beforehand, then slice them and put them on the dough, otherwise they will be too raw.

Pizza *Margherita*

1 quantity pizza dough
(see page 204)

1 x 400 g (14 oz) can Italian
peeled tomatoes

1 fresh large mozzarella
or 6 ovolini

6–8 fresh basil leaves

2 cloves garlic, crushed

salt and freshly ground
black pepper

olive oil

Preheat oven to 240°C (460°F). Roll out some dough on to an oiled oven tray – the dough should be about ½ cm (¼ in) thick. Spread garlic on this base.

Drain tomatoes of their juice and seeds and chop roughly. Add to base, then break the mozzarella into little pieces and spread evenly on top of tomatoes. Tear the basil leaves and put over pizza, then add salt and pepper.

Lastly, sprinkle some olive oil over the whole pizza. Cook in oven for about 10–15 minutes or until base is coloured and crunchy, or in a pizza oven for 3–5 minutes.

Pizza

PROSCIUTTO E *Ruggola*

PROSCIUTTO AND ARUGULA PIZZA

**1 quantity pizza dough
(see page 204)**

**1 x 400 g (14 oz) can Italian
peeled tomatoes**

**1 small can (about 150 g/5 oz)
tomato paste (optional)**

1–2 cloves garlic, crushed

1 chilli, finely sliced

**100 g (3½ oz) prosciutto di
Parma, left in long slices**

virgin olive oil

**1 bunch arugula (rocket)
leaves, roughly chopped**

50 g (2 oz) piece of parmigiano

**Maldon sea salt and freshly
ground black pepper**

Preheat oven to 240°C (460°F). Roll out some pizza dough on an oiled oven tray. It should not be thicker than ½ cm (¼ in).

Drain tomatoes of all their liquid. Chop them roughly, drain again: the tomatoes should not be wet. You can add the tomato concentrate to make the taste stronger.

Spread garlic and chilli evenly on the pizza base, add the tomatoes and then some prosciutto.

Drizzle a little olive oil over the pizza.

Cook in the very hot conventional oven for about 5–10 minutes, or in a pizza oven if you have one for about 3–5 minutes, until bottom of base is coloured and crunchy.

Take out of the oven. With a potato peeler, slice some parmigiano over the pizza and, lastly, top with the arugula. Then drizzle some more virgin olive oil over the pizza and grind some black pepper on top and salt if needed.

Pizza Napoletana

NEAPOLITAN PIZZA

1 quantity pizza dough
(see page 204)

1 small can (about 150 g/5 oz)
tomato paste

1–2 cloves garlic, crushed

1 chilli, sliced (optional)

1 x 400 g (14 oz) can Italian
peeled tomatoes

18–20 anchovies

handful of pitted good olives

2 tablespoons capers

freshly ground black pepper

fresh oregano

virgin olive oil

Preheat oven to 240°C (460°F).

Roll out dough to ½ cm (¼ in) thick and put on an oiled oven tray. Spread some tomato paste on base, then some garlic and chilli. Drain tomatoes very well, discard seeds and roughly break tomatoes with your fingers, spreading evenly over the dough. Then add the anchovies, arranging them diagonally on the pizza base. (If you buy the ones in salt, wash them very well to remove all salt, then pat dry; good quality anchovies in oil can also be used.)

Add the olives, capers and ground pepper (be careful if you add any salt as the anchovies are already salted), some fresh oregano and a drizzle of olive oil.

Bake in oven for about 5–10 minutes in a conventional oven, 3–5 minutes in a pizza oven, or until pizza base is crispy.

Digestivi

JUST FOR THE STOMACH

EARLIER IN THIS BOOK WE OPENED THE EVENING WITH APERITIVI, BOTH A drink and a ritual, and now we need to close the evening in the same way. 'Digestivi', or digestive liqueurs, are an important part of the Italian dining experience and, of course, you have the gentle suggestion, if it helps to think this way, that you are drinking them not out of indulgence but for your digestion.

On one occasion I was offered a digestivo and protested that, much as I would like to, my head the next day would not allow it. The response, quick as a flash, was 'But, Signora, the head can look after itself. You must look after the stomach!'

As with aperitivi, the decision regarding location is important. Mostly I prefer to go on from where we have been having dinner, to a café or bar and have a digestivo with coffee there. The exception is at da Tito in San Pantaleo, where Tito has an extensive range of home-made digestivi.

Italian digestivi are less well known than the aperitivi but no less original. The classic tradition is the 'amaro', or bitter. Derived probably from old monastic recipes, the bitter drinks have been sweetened over time to soften their impact. The exceptions are Fernet-Branca and Averna, which are very bitter, almost medicinal – acquired tastes. But they do seem exactly right when a big dinner sits heavily on the

stomach. Apart from the amari, grappa, the spirit distilled from the leftovers of wine crushing, is widely drunk. And there is a large collection of special sweet liqueurs like Sambucco, Galliano or Liquore Strega.

On this trip we did something I have never done before — we had a digestivo tasting of Tito's home-made liqueurs. There was a fragrant grappa (mown hay with a light floral undertone), limoncello (that citrus scent of summer), latte di capra (made from distilled goats' milk), mirto (the Sardegnan liqueur made from myrtle berries) and nocino (made from fresh walnuts). This was a serious range of choices, so great care was taken to taste them a number of times for comparison purposes and it was accompanied by lots of swallowing and no spitting. Our favourite was the limoncello so I have included my recipe for limoncello in this chapter.

The most unusual to the modern taste is probably the latte di capra. Who would have thought a liqueur made from goats' milk would be drinkable? The taste is unusual — fairly sweet with a little whiff of goat up the nose along the way. Looking through Nonnino's recipes I came across his version of this digestive which was known, in the Lugano of his time, to be a favourite tipple of old women. So I have included a similar recipe using cows' milk. I admit it's unusual, an acquired taste if you like, but you might be inspired to try it.

In Sardegna the grappa is also distinctive and particularly good. It comes from an old tradition. The most popular brand is called Filo di Ferro, literally 'wire grappa'. This is not a reflection on the taste, but an historical reference to the times when the best and strongest grappa would be heavily taxed, even if you made it yourself. So the home-made grappa was attached to a wire and hung down the well. When the customs and excise officials arrived to search for it, there was none to be found. Presumably the well water also cooled the grappa which, to my mind, in summer is best drunk icy cold by putting the bottle, and sometimes the glasses, in the freezer section of the refrigerator.

If you go to one of the cafés in the Porto Cervo piazza after dinner for your digestivo, the passegiata is in full swing again. There is probably a lull over the dinner hours, then it's all action as the night swells with colour and movement.

It's fun also to go to the port. There is a particular café/bar there called Bar del Porto, right behind the wharf. It has been there since the beginning of the Costa Smeralda and is a favourite haunt for the crews as well as for a few of the more adventurous owners. Bar del Porto opens early and is a good spot at breakfast to

The memorable digestivi tasting at Ristorante da Tito.

observe the comings and goings as the boats are made ready for the day's outing. It's also good in the early evening to have an aperitivo under the branches of an old spreading fig tree which faintly, but distinctly, scents the night air. And it's a great place to go for your digestivo after dinner. Wide divans looking out over the port line the walls, the backgammon sets are out, the digestivi are many and various and there is usually a crowd settling in for the evening. From there they will probably go to one of the Costa Smeralda's celebrated night clubs, like the Sotto Vento, or the subtly named Billionaire. The people and the gossip-rich goings-on in these clubs are widely followed in certain sections of the Italian press, usually accompanied by pictures – showing the tell-tale fuzz of a long lens – of the same people in states of undress enjoying themselves on the open sun-decks of large boats.

So, however you are planning to spend your evening, the digestivo is essential to settle the stomach for whatever happens later on.

Limoncello

4 lemons, organic, not sprayed

1 litre (2 pints) vodka

1 cup caster (superfine) sugar

500 ml (1 pint) water

juice of 1 lemon

Soak lemons in water for about 30 minutes. Dry them and peel off all the skin, being careful not to cut any of the white of the lemon with the peel (the pith will make the limoncello bitter).

Put lemon peel and 2 cups vodka into a jar and let stand for 4 days.

Make a syrup with sugar and water. When cool, add to the lemon peel and alcohol. Add the remaining alcohol plus juice of 1 lemon. Let stand in a dark place for another 4 days.

Now pass through a filter. Let it stand for at least another week before drinking.

Latte DI Vecchia

500 ml (17 fl oz) whole milk

1 kg (2 lb 3 oz) caster (superfine) sugar

1 litre (2 pints) grappa or vodka (see Note)

1 lemon, sliced in rounds

2 whole vanilla beans, chopped and ground with 3 teaspoons sugar

Put everything into an airtight, sterilised glass jar. Let it stand in a dark place for 20 days, shaking the glass every day. Now pass it through a filter and pour into sterilised bottles. The liqueur will separate if left standing for a long time: just shake the bottle before serving.

Note

Tito makes this digestivo with goats' milk. This is my grandfather's version, and he used organic whole cows' milk instead.

In the original recipe, 95% pure alcohol is used instead of grappa or vodka! The amount of milk then would double, so you would use 1 litre (2 pints) whole milk.

Mirto

600 g (1 lb 5 oz) myrtle berries

1 litre (2 pints) alcohol (90%)
or if not available, grappa

600 g (1 lb 5 oz) honey

water

Put myrtle berries in alcohol, cover and leave in a dark place for about 8 days. Strain it and discard the berries.

Dissolve honey in water: if using 90% alcohol add 2 litres water; if using grappa, 1 litre water. Add to myrtle-flavoured alcohol. Leave in a dark place for another 8 days.

Inspiration
AND MEMORIES, SOTTO
La Pergola

I AM BACK HOME IN SYDNEY AND THE MEMORIES OF THE TRIP TO LUGANO AND Sardegna are just a warm glow. Every time I return there, apart from the sheer enjoyment of it all and seeing my family again, I find new inspiration, new ideas to follow up.

Although the food and way of life I have enjoyed in these weeks were those of Lugano and the Costa Smeralda, you can live and eat this way in many parts of the world: in warmer climates for much of the year, while in colder places it is great for those warm summer days. Sydney, like many other places in the world, has an excellent climate for my favourite al fresco life. We have mild winters when, if you are sheltered from the wind and the sun is out, it is warm enough to eat outside in the middle of the day. In summer it may be too warm – it depends on what shade you have – but then the nights are possible. There is nothing quite like eating outside by candlelight on a balmy evening.

At home in Sydney we have a large pergola attached to the house so we can live al fresco as often as possible. The roof of the pergola has a wisteria growing over it but we have also lined it with fine bamboo slatted panels. The same material has been made into blinds which can be lowered to take the glare off a hot midday sun.

Left: The monster from the deep – this is a red emperor.

Above left: Jason presents the Pesce al Sale. My younger son Daniel is in the background. Above right: Cracking the crust. Far right: Preparing the salt crust.

Under the pergola are two large outdoor tables and benches. I like nothing better than to prepare a Sunday lunch for my family and friends which can be spread the length of the tables in this idyllic setting. It is our equivalent to the roof terrace in Sardegna, the olive tree in Lugano or the walled garden in Tehran.

The food, of course, is the sort of food we have been enjoying on our travels. It is the right food for the way we live; relaxed, unstuffy, simple to prepare and very much to your personal taste. The food is spread in platters and bowls all over the table and everyone helps themselves. It is our version of Tito's grand antipasto.

On a warm day in late spring, not long after I returned from my trip, I made such a lunch and on the following page is what I made.

Sotto la Pergola

Menu

Antipasto

Polipi con Patate (Page 188)

Peperoni con Acciughe (Page 187)

Acciughe Fresche (Page 184)

Antipasto di Cozze (Page 183)

Fogli di Musica (page 114)

Pesce al Sale con Olio e Limone (page 191)

Carcioffi Crudi con Parmigiano (page 117)

Insalata di Faggiolini (page 93)

Insalata di Canelli (page 199)

Sorbetto di Pompelmo Rosa con Campari (page 18)

RECIPE INDEX

Manuela Darling-Gansser was born in Lugano, Switzerland. She spent her early childhood in Iran before returning to school in Zurich. An inveterate traveller and keen linguist, she has lived at times in the USA, Japan, Italy and the UK, and visited other parts of Asia, India and north Africa. She has been a passionate cook all her life.

Simon Griffiths is a leading photographer of garden, food and travel. He has undertaken overseas assignments for *Australian Gourmet Traveller* and his work appears regularly in other magazines such as *House and Garden* and *Vogue Living*. He was the photographer for the *Tuscan Cookbook*, *Salute* and *Walking the Dog in Italy*.